GO ALL THE WAY

A SELF MASTERY HANDBOOK FOR ALL

Michaela,
May you go all
the way with
your deepest goals
& desires!

Love & Light
Matthew
Dae
2017

By: Mahkah Das

(Nicols Samuel Florino)

ISBN - 13: 978-1542423748

ISBN-10: 1542423740

I dedicate this book to all who want joy and peace in their lives. It is for all who seek ultimate freedom and happiness. It is for those who want to master the body, mind, and the energies of universal law to live out their true life purpose. May this book assist in the transition from being a slave of conditions to unconditional love, clarity, and alignment. This is for you.

"The way out...is in."

- SADHGURU

: CONTENTS :

PART III

A NOTE TO READER

This book is intended to be a guide to mastering your mind, body, and energies. This means that you will become the master of your life by learning how to control your thoughts, emotions, sensations, and energy that you feel in your day to day life. You will gain the knowledge and tools to manage and maintain balance in your body. You will be offered practices to help you feel good, which means deeper peace of mind, vitality, energy, clarity, and all around happiness. You can over come long lasting negative emotions and trauma. You can heal past and present mental, emotional, or physical wounds. You can transform your life in any way you wish. You can achieve anything you desire. If you desire it, it can manifest and become a reality to you. This is a handbook on how to be a human being. This is a "how to" guide for living life to the fullest. This is what we all should have learned in school. These practices and teachings are a simplified summary of what all the great saints, monks, sages, and spiritual masters have taught and are continuing to teach.

LET IT BE KNOWN/WARNING

* The practices and teachings in this book are not intended to cure or treat any medically diagnosed illnesses, diseases, or conditions. These practices and teachings are not intended to replace any medication or current practice for any disease or medical condition.
* If you are unsure if you should be practicing what is offered in this book, please consult your local trusted

spiritual teacher or health care adviser before attempting to do the practices suggested in this book.

* These practices and way of preserving life are real and are universal truths. Applying what is suggested in this book to your life can make major shifts happen in your life. Your entire life may turn upside down. Things might start happing to you that are extreme in nature and possibly uncomfortable. Know that this is what waking up looks like. It is highly encouraged that you practice what is suggested in this book with a teacher/guru who understands what is stated in this book and can help you integrate what is being offered. Go at your own pace. Take it easy and slow. If you are meant to go fast, it will happen by itself. There is no rush. Be kind to yourself. Are you ready to transform into the fullness of who you are and why you have come? If you are holding this book in your hands...you are ready.

I wish you ease and grace on your journey home.

- MAHKAH DAS

: INTRO & PART 1 :

In the Introduction I share a little of my life's journey and how I got to where I am now. Part One goes into living life in the "Now" and what that means. You will learn how your mind works and master the Law Of Attraction, the greatest law in the universe. Understanding the Law Of Attraction allows you to live the life you truly want, and get all the things you want in this lifetime!

: Intro :

MY LIFE...SO FAR

I'm going to be brief and to the point here. There is no need to dwell on the past. I came into this human life named Nicolas Samuel Florino to a supportive, loving and open-minded family. I have the most caring and supportive parents I could ever dream of. Since I was a kid, I knew I was put onto this Earth to do something massive and special with my life. I have always felt great power within me, but never knew what to do with it. Growing up I had many questions about the meaning of life. My parents and family have taught me so much. They imparted priceless teachings that shaped who I am as a human on this Earth. My two older brothers, Chris and Tino, are intelligent, talented, beautiful, funny, awesome souls. My parents and brothers demonstrated a different way of living life on this planet, especially in America. I learned to be a kind and caring human being, to follow my passions, and enjoy this life to the fullest. I will always look up to them.

I am blessed to have known many wise teachers, counsellors, therapists, energy healers and shamans throughout my life. I have studied with some of the most respected yogic teachers and philosophers of our time. I have studied and practiced various religions and belief systems including Christianity, Buddhism, Tantra, Wicca, Paganism,

Shamanism, Native American practices, Satanism, Hinduism, and much more. I have studied in depth the teachings of masters such as Abraham Hicks, B.K.S. Iyengar, Ram Dass, Eckhart Tolle, Thich Nhat Hanh, His Holiness the Dalai Lama, Bhagavan Das, Sadhguru, and Deepak Chopra. I am a certified Hatha yoga teacher with countless hours of practice in yoga asana, pranayama, meditation, mantra, and philosophy. I am also a certified Reiki Master. However, out of all my teachers and guides on this Earth, my sister Deneene has been the one to show me the true spiritual side of things ever since I was a young boy. I benefit from her life experience since she is 20 years older than me. Anything I have gone through, she experienced in some way also. My sister also studied several religions and spiritual practices throughout her life, ranging from various modalities of energy work, psychic work, past life and death work, spirit/ ghost work, energy clearing, to over 10 years of service in hospice care. She is an author and a practicing Buddhist. My sister taught me what it means to be spiritual and how to create my own spiritually, to live life mindfully with compassion, and that everything is energy. Most importantly, she taught me how to meditate at a very young age. I thank my entire family for always supporting and sharing with me their wisdom and knowledge about life, and for their unconditional love and support.

I'll share a little more about my past. I played competitive hockey from age 8 to 16. I was told I was very good. I dedicated my life to it, and it showed. However, I eventually found myself at a crossroads where for the very first time I faced a major life changing decision: either continue playing hockey and become a professional player, or pursue a life of sex, drugs, and rock n' roll. So on September 11, 2001, I decided to quit hockey, for my heart wasn't in it anymore. I was doing it more for my father who was my biggest support and fan. I remember crying and telling him why I wanted to quit. His response was, "Son, I will always support you and love you no matter what." He has stayed true to that love and support. That was the first time in my life when I really listened to my heart and gut, which has never steered me wrong.

From age 15 to 21, I experimented with women, drugs, and the rock star lifestyle. I smoked copious amounts of weed and experimented with mind-altering substances. By age 21 however, I was so sensitive to my body I could feel that I was killing myself with cigarettes and other drugs. My body was crying out "Stop it Nick!" I listened and in 2006 I quit everything cold turkey. I asked my sister what could I do to move on and heal the damage. She suggested yoga. My life transformed dramatically. Yoga literally saved my life, and at that point I began a life of spiritual practice. I intuitively knew there was more to life than what I was experiencing. So I went for it and made my first big dive into my inner world.

I have never felt like I fit into American society. I always felt very different from my peers and friends. I thought that I had to be something or do something with my life like everyone else, but I never really knew what that was. I grew up with Attention Deficit Disorder and had trouble reading and writing. I attended a private school, Cove School, from the 3rd to 8th grade. Cove taught me how to read, write, focus, how to be my true self, and interact with people in a positive way. Thank you, Cove, and all my teachers. Thank you Mom and Dad for having the awareness and courage to put me in a "special school." Going to Cove really showed me how to feel compassion and true love for all beings.

In addition to feeling different on the inside, I also felt like I had to show this by expressing it outwardly through my clothing and music. I have tried experimenting with every stereotype you can think of: from hippie to preppie, from skater-punk with dreads to Marilyn Manson obsessed Satanic goth, and everything in between! You name it, I have tried to identify with it. None of them really stuck for too long, as I intuitively knew that it was a process of forming my identity and deciding for myself what I like and what I don't like. It's like going to a ice cream shop and trying all the flavors just because you can! Why not? So from much trial and error, trying to be this person and that person, trying to fit into this category or that way of living, I found something beneficial from my life experience. The only thing that ever stayed with me was my spiritual practice, which means being a mindful and loving human being who is always learning and wanting to help others grow and expand. Who I am is not what I wear, or what job I have. What's important is who I am inside and that I project myself outwardly to the world in positive, balanced, and mindful way. I soon realized after starting yoga and diving deep into meditation and my spiritual work, that everything is a balance between doing my inner and outer work. The inner work consists of retreating and withdrawing internally to pray, meditate, listen and being still. The outer work involves sharing knowledge and helping people heal, grow, and live out their life's true purpose. Life is a balance of retreating and going inward, and then returning to the world to teach, share and enjoy life together. I discovered my purpose as a teacher. And I have realized that we all are artists with gifts to share.

This book is another way I can share what I have known to be true and what has worked for me on my journey. Anyone can be spiritual and find enlightenment in this lifetime by simply making a choice. Everyone can customize their life, especially their spiritual practice. This is the main subject of this book: How to create your own spiritual practice. There is no one way to live this life, there are endless ways. The same is true for spirituality and the decision to be enlightened. Many paths lead to the same place, and anyone can awaken in this lifetime. I am here to inspire you to find clarity and peace in your life. Any pain you may feel inside can go away. You can heal, learn from, and let go of all that is holding you back from being your true self, no matter how bad or horrible or big you think it is. Peace, ease and clarity is attainable, for it is already within you. It never goes away. It's always there waiting for you to realize it. When you do claim the peace within, life opens its doors to you in ways you never thought possible, allowing you to follow your dreams and passions. The life you dream of will be more than just a dream; it will manifest into a reality.

People often need guidance or help to release the unwanted stuff inside, and to fully live the life they desire. We come into this life in one of two different ways. The first is is the quick and easy way, which is to be born with the "light on." These beings come into the world knowing the truth about Source, life, energy, and mindfulness from the

14

get-go. No path needs to be laid for them, no teacher needs to give them a map. They just know. This is rare, but it does happen. The other way is how most humans are born. We go from knowing the truth as kids, to unlearning it as we grow up. Then hopefully, through living life and doing our inner work, we awaken back to the truth of who we are and why we are here. We realize there is more to this life than just going to school, getting a job, getting married, having kids, paying bills, collecting things, growing old, and then dying. We forget the truth and need assistants, a method or methods, or a map to return to the truth and freedom we all desire. When we enter this body we innately know the truth of who we are and why we are here, but we forget this truth over the course of our lives. We can restore this knowledge through a process of unlearning and relearning, but usually we need a teacher to guide us through it. This is the process of customizing your spiritual practices.

This book is meant to be a tool to reawaken who you are and why you have come here, and to discover what you're all about. Its purpose is to help you customize and create a spiritual practice that works for you, your lifestyle, and desires. You have to personalize your spiritual practice to your everyday life, where you live, and your intentions. Even if you believe to have found enlightenment already, there will be something for you here, I promise. We are never done expanding and learning. I will share with you what I have known to be true thus far in my own journey. I will only share with you that which I know to be true for me. Some parts may resonate with you, and other parts will make no sense. Take and leave what you wish. This will be a book that you can read once, and then get something completely new out of it if you come back to it years later. We connect to, and resonate with, what we are ready to experience in our lives at that precise moment.

Let us awaken and expand together, on this magic carpet ride of life on planet Earth. This life is meant to be extremely fun! You did not come here just to suffer and get by. We are all Divine creators, who possess the power to create worlds. When we perceive life as fun, and when we feel good now, it will seem as though everything in your life and the universe just falls into place. This is the peace, ease, and clarity I spoke of earlier.

: 1 :

REMEMBERING WHO YOU REALLY ARE & WHY YOU HAVE COME

Many people identify who they are with their thoughts, mind, body, and ego or personality. These aspects are just a fraction of the endless ocean of who we really are. You are not your mind. You are not your body. You are not your ego. You have a mind, a body, and a personality, but this is not who you really are. This is simply a case of mistaken identity. All these aspects are a part of being human on Earth, but they are not truly who we are at the core of our being. My experience has shown me that we are vibrational energetic beings who live in a vibrational energetic time-space reality. We have living within us that which humans call "God," "Source," "The Divine Mother," "Jah," "Spirit," "Ma," use whatever word you like. I connect with the words "Source" and "Ma" to describe the vibrational energetic divine life force energy that lives in all living things. Most people call this energy "God." We are pure and loving Source energy residing in a body here on Earth. We are a slice of the pie, so to speak. We are on Earth to create whatever we want to in that moment, while also experiencing pleasure in the act of creating and co-creating together. We are vibrationally connected to everyone and every living thing on Earth, and throughout the entire universe. We are sacred, divine creators who are on Earth to grow, have fun, and, feel good. Period. That's really what this whole healing and spiritual trip comes down to. We have come to mindfully and deliberately experience whatever we want, from moment to moment. Look at the children and the animals, they still remember this truth! You are made up of the same force that created the world, your body, and the universe. Consciousness, awareness, and presence is all Source energy. You are that which you feel when you feel love for something or someone. You are the Divine itself. Pure love.

We have been given our bodies and minds to help us attain what we want and to experience the joy of achieving our desires, whether that is a cup of coffee, making love to our lover, or being a millionaire. We have all come as powerful creator-Gods to shape our own blissful reality. This experience is intended to be enjoyable, like a life-long vacation. Yeah I said it, and I believe it! Earth is heaven, and we are Gods! Man has done a good job of forgetting about all this. We come into our physical bodies knowing this truth, and forget it as we age. We are blessed with magical imaginations to envision and dream about what we want to experience and have, simply for the pleasurable feeling of having it. We are all skillful at make-believe. Kids do it all the time, but usually they pretend to be a monster, or a fairy, or a superhero in some make-believe world of play and fun. We "grow up" and use our wonderful imaginations to create mostly unwanted things in our life. You decide you want something, but then realize that you don't have it. You then focus most of your attention on the absence of that thing, which makes you feel bad. That emotion of feeling bad creates more negative things to feel bad about. We tend to focus on unwanted things and figure out how things are going to happen. We are obsessed with trying to figure it out! It really is sick. Recently however, people are waking up and shifting their thoughts to focus on what they do want, instead of what they don't. Again, everything is vibrational energy.

We are all brought into being by the Divine Creator, who is an artist. Look at the beauty they are creating! Therefore, we are creators and artists also. Earth is full of artists. Walk into a room filled with young kids and ask them, "Who here is an artist?" They will probably all raise their hands. We are here to create whatever it is that brings us pleasure. We came into this life to have fun and feel good! That is what it all comes down to, my friends. We are here to have fun, create, and feel good. Period. We have lost our way somehow, and have gone a little off course. So many people think life is all about getting an education in order to to get the high paying job so that they can get all the stuff and save up money to retire, and then do all the things they wish they did when they were younger. People work so hard their entire lives for they want, but never really have the time to enjoy it because they are so busy being busy. Then one day, while you're so busy, you die. It's interesting if you think about it, isn't it? This does not sound fun to me! If you are one of the many people living this way, and are reading this book, then you know there has to be something else to this life. You're right! You can go to school and learn about something you are very passionate about. You can work a job that you are passionate about. You can marry someone who is beautiful in every way, and have a healthy powerful relationship. You can have kids and a career, and do it all while staying connected to what really makes you happy.

What do you love? What really turns you on? What brightens your eyes and lights you up inside? We all have something that we love, a dream or a passion. I am here, like many masters before me, to tell you to follow your bliss. Follow your dream, follow your passion and make it into a reality now! Forget about this preplanned lifestyle of settling for less than what you really want. So many people are working jobs and living a life they don't want because they think this is just how life is. They feel as if there is no other option. "Everyone else I know is doing this so I must be doing something right?" No! Stop living a life of regret. You create your own reality. Bhagavan Das told us to "Live this birth for all it's worth!" Now is the time to do what you want and enjoy this beautiful gift of life. What if this is it? What if you don't get another chance to come back to Earth! If you are reading this, that means you have been given the gift of human life to enjoy and be the artist that you are. Your whole life can be a vacation! This is the leading edge of all that is. This is heaven. Source is here on Earth, dwelling within all living things, just waiting for you to recognize her. Source loves to be appreciated. For appreciation and love, which is really the same thing, is all that is.

If you can look at a tree, and see yourself in that tree, and feel the love and light from that tree within yourself, then you are beginning to understand who you really are. Pure, positive, Source energy. No matter what your life looks like now, you can change it. Yes, you can. No matter what age you are, or what state your physical body and mind are in. No matter what type of relationship you're involved in, or your financial situation; you have the power to shift anything you want and experience it fully in this lifetime. What do you think all these healers, saints, and sages were trying to teach us? They are no different then you and me. Jesus, the Buddha, all the mystic teachers, healers, saints and sages are humans too. They merely found a way to connect to Source often and focus purely on what they want, while in alignment with who they really are. They mastered releasing resistance and found peace in their minds and hearts. You can live in this state too. The masters are here to show us what is humanly possible.

Most of us have lived many lives on Earth and other planets. By living all these lives we have discovered what things we want or don't want, which creates contrast. Contrast is our best friend. From knowing what we don't want, we realize what we do want. My father taught me this at a very young age. Being cold makes you appreciate being warm. Being hungry makes you appreciate eating good food. I don't like rap music, I do like rock music. I don't like mean people, I like happy people. And so on and so forth. You get this, yes? Through living out your lives, you determine personal preferences. You, sometimes unknowingly, give lists to the universe of what you do and do not want. When you decide on what you want, it instantly manifests vibrationally, waiting for you to line up with the vibrational emotion of it. What exactly does this mean and how do you line up with it? First, you have to understand what your core desires are. Everything you want, no matter what it is, is for the same one reason: you want it because you think by having it you will feel good, better than you already do now. There are simple ways to receive all of the things you have decided that you want. Creation, and getting what you want, comes down to mastering the greatest law of the universe, the Law Of Attraction.

: 2 :

UNDERSTANDING THE LAW OF ATTRACTION

Everyone and everything is energy. You live in a vibrational reality. You are more than the physical body you can see with your eyes. You are more than your senses. You are more than your thoughts. You know this now. Part of your spirit dwells in the body, and the other larger part is still pure vibrational energy in pure alignment with Source. I know what you're saying: "Yeah yeah yeah, I get it, but what about all the money I want?!" So how do you get all those things you want? Imagine a stick. One end of this stick is what you want, the other end of the stick is what you don't want. Everything comes down to which end of the stick you are giving most of your attention via your thoughts, words, and visualization. This mental imagery creates feelings within you. So you either focus your attention on the feeling of having what you want, or the feeling of not having it. You want the nice car, the beautiful lover, lots of money, a fit healthy body, the perfect business, and so on. Whatever it is, know it has already manifested in vibrational form. Whatever you decide you want, you can have. No exception. This is why we come to Earth, to experience aligning with the vibration of what we want, and experience those desires in fully manifested physical form.

You're still saying, "Yeah yeah yeah, how do I get my stuff?" It's simple. Feel good. "That's it? There has be to more than that!" Simply put my friends, that's it! There is a little catch to this however. The Law of Attraction responds to how you feel, not just your thoughts. At first you might say, "Okay, I will think happy thoughts, and I will get everything I want." As many masters have said, you are not just your thoughts. You can think all day long of things that feel good, but what you are really reaching for is a positive emotional feeling. It is that feeling of love in your heart, or that gut feeling that comes from the emotional high and excitement of thinking about what you want. You have to feel wonderful, not just think wonderful thoughts. The words in your head are just words, and yes, at first they can help bring you to a place of emotionally feeling good. But the key is to do anything in the world that makes you feel good. Another way of saying this is: get happy! Pet your dog, listen to music you love, eat some yummy food, make love to your beloved, watch a funny movie, go for a walk, read a good book. Do anything to feel good. You want to find a place of unconditionally feeling good within you first, and then thought and action will come in the form of a powerful impulse that will assist in moving you towards your desires. You must feel your way through life, rather than just think and act. Words and actions alone have no power. When you have that positive, loving feeling of worthiness and vitality within you, combined with a strong clear intention, then the perfect action will happen on its own every moment.

Try not to overthink this teaching. There is no need to figure out with words in your mind the thing that you want to improve or have. Source has already figured it out for you. When you ask for something it is instantly and vibrationally given to you. So all you have to do is line up the vibrational feeling of what you want. I know some of you are saying, "Well if I can have this thing that I want now, I would feel so much better. If I had this amount of money, or if I lived there, or if I was in this relationship, or if I had this type of body, then I would feel good." I get it, I used to think that same way. Give me this and I will feel good. Give me this and I will feel better. The key realization here is to flip this around. Feel good now, with the physical absence of the thing you want, and what you want has to come. It is law. Another way of saying this is to find unconditional happiness. Not needing something outside of you to make you happy. Not needing conditions to make you happy. It's really not the car, or the money, or the relationship you want. It's about the emotional feeling of what it is like to have what you want. No matter what it is. It's the feeling of being alive, excited, clear, and full of vitality, power and love! That's really what you want. To feel good. To feel happy. To feel alive!

Now I'm not saying that you shouldn't want things. The physical and sensory enjoyment of your desires is part of being human on Earth. If you want something you should have it, and you surely deserve it all. Figure out the emotional feeling of what you want, and feel it as fully as possible throughout your day; what you want has to come. Use any subject in the world that feels good, even if it is unrelated to the subject of what you want in that moment. Like attracts like. Life will help you decide what you want by knowing what you don't want. "I feel sad" you might say, but you know you want to be happy. So when you feel negative emotion about something, stop and ask yourself in that moment how you would rather feel. If I don't want this, then what do I want? That's when you start to look for the emotions you are really seeking. Emotions like, "I feel alive, I feel clear, I feel excited, I want to have fun, I want to feel love," and so on. Notice that I stated my desire in the present tense as though it is already happening, rather than reaching for it in the future. This is very important. Another example is that you want a lot of money, yes? Why? Because you really want to have fun and feel good. Okay, so have fun and feel good now in this moment, even though presently you may not have a lot of money. Soon all that money will come because you are feeling the emotional sensation of what you want. Why? Because everything in this universe is vibration, including your emotions. When your emotions become one with the vibrational emotion linked to money, by law the money has to come to you. That's it. Replace money with anything you desire, and you've got it. It's a practice. The first part of manifestation is the feeling, and soon after comes the physical form.

How soon you desire becomes a physically manifested reality depends on your consistent positive attitude and alignment with the emotional vibration of your desire. This is a practice, and like all practices you have to keep it up and stay focused. It is like driving a car on a long road trip. You as the driver have to stay focused enough to stay on the road to get from point A to point B safely. There may be traffic, there may be bumps on the road, there may be unwanted weather, but you stay on the road and get to your destination. You don't stop the car or pull over and quit just because things get difficult. Some people might but you will not. This manifestation process is the same. You have to stay focused on the goal, and do your best every day in every moment. Do this and you will be greatly rewarded.

I know this might be a little out there for some of you. But I am living proof that these laws and practices work. You must do your best to feel as good as you can in every moment, no matter what your current state is. When you consistently find this place of feeling good, all that you want will come to you. By living this way you are always in the present moment, not wishing something was different all the time. There is no need to always try and fix something, or do something to make something else happen. This is called "deliberate creation." You are no longer creating by default. You now know that everything you desire is already created vibrationally. Everything is done and waiting for you to align with it. Let it be done, trust that it's done, and focus on feeling good. No matter what. If you begin every day with the intention to feel good and have fun, and really mean it, I promise your life will transform in ways you never knew were possible. But you have to actually do it and feel it. Nobody can do this for you. Other people can't truly make you happy. Things can't make you happy. You have to find it within yourself, the love, the joy of being alive. Let go of the need for another person or thing to fulfill or complete you. Practice this, and watch what happens. This is all you really need to know. Feel good, and have fun. Everyday that is my main intention. Everything else I leave to God, and I feel more alive than I ever thought was possible. Again, it does take some practice. It might be a slow process for you, or it might be quick. Again, this life experience is a very personal one. You can't compare your problems or desires to anybody else's. This is your journey, and it's all about how your own path unfolds. It isn't about the thing you think you want. It's about the path that leads you there, and the feeling of fun, joy, and expansion along the way.

Enjoy everything and everyone. It is possible to go from a state of appreciation, to a state of joy, to a state of fun, to a state of excitement, to a state of surprise, to a state of pleasure everyday, all day! We are living on this Earth to thrive and create and love. On the flip side, some people say that desire is a path to suffering, and on some levels it can be. If you expect situations, things, and people to fulfill you and make you happy it will never work. This is when desire can bring suffering or make you broke, which brings more suffering. The Law Of Attraction works both ways, bringing you whatever you focus on constantly. If you feel bad, you get more "bad." If you feel good, you get more "good." You decide you want something, realize you don't have it, and then feel negative emotion because you don't have it. By focusing attention on unwanted or negative feelings, the universe brings you more things to feel bad about. More and more things to feel bad about makes you feel worse and worse, which leads to thought-induced suffering. People live like this all over the world. When you are uncomfortable and suffering, you buy more things, eat more food, develop an addiction, talk about how bad your life is, and how you don't have this or that. Whatever you give your attention to, you direct energy there. Whether it is wanted or unwanted. The Law of Attraction gives you more of what you focus on and feel emotionally. So if you can retrain your mind to focus on what is wanted, instead of what is unwanted, then you will get what you want! Done! Over. That's it! It's like a game. You catch those unwanted feelings or negative thoughts in the   moment, then change your thoughts and focus continuously on something that feels good. This way of thinking and practice can be mastered by seated meditation which I go over in Chapter 8. I recommend not skipping ahead until you have read this book completely at least once. These teachings are given in a specific order for optimal understanding and clarity.

You are guided and protected, my friends. You have angels, spirits, animal guides, warriors, past relatives, sages and saints guiding you and protecting you. They are always shining a light on everything you want. Here it is, it's over here! Come this way! Think about this! The guidance is always there. Most importantly, we each have a guidance system within us that shows us the easiest and quickest path to our desires. This guidance system is your emotions and your impulses which live in your gut, or the solar plexus. Here is one way to connect to your guidance system. If you have a question on your mind, ask your guidance system or guides if it is a "yes" or a "no." If the answer is "yes," you will get a "fuck yes!" feeling. If your impulse says "maybe," that means "no." If the answer is "no," then it will be a strong "no!" Trust yourself. It all comes down to paying attention to the moment and living life mindfully. Your emotions tell you if your answer is a "yes" or "no" as well. If the answer you get feels wonderful inside you, it's a "yes." If the answer you feel creates a negative response, then "no." Figuring something out can be that simple. Why complicate things? You have to chill out more! You have to slow down and calm down. Balance and center yourself. Go beyond the noise of your thoughts and get out of your way! This takes work, desire, and focus. For most people, deep work is needed to master this practice and way of living. Don't let this discourage you. We all have stuff that gets in the way of mindful living and finding peace. If you're in pain, you have to release that pain. If you have an image, or story, or past experience in your mind that won't go away and makes you feel like crap every time you think about it, you have to work on it and let it go. In the following chapters, I will talk about different ways to release the unwanted and help you become present in the now. The present moment is where all of life exists, and where everything you want lives. First, you must learn how your unique mind works, and practice mastering it!

: 3 :

MASTERING YOUR MIND!

We are blessed to live in a time when we have ready access to the wisdom, teachings, and potent knowledge of past and present spiritual masters. Many books have been written on living life in the present moment. The one I connected to the most was The Power Of Now by Eckhart Tolle. As he and others have stated many times: "Life is all happening now." There is no other time than the Now. The past is done. The future never really comes. When it does come, it happens now. If you can wrap your mind around this truth, life becomes a lot less hectic and stressful. When you close your eyes and take a few gentle deep breaths, and feel your breath as you inhale and exhale, your mind goes from thinking, which is involved in time, to the present moment, the Now. The "you" that is watching and feeling your breath is not thought. It's not thinking. Close you eyes and feel your breath for a few moments. Think to yourself, who is the "I" that is feeling my breath? Go ahead now! I dare you!

You see, the mind always wants to be thinking. One main function of the human brain is to produce thought, just like every other organ does something specific for the body to live. Many people are trained to believe in and focus on every thought that comes and goes. How much harm and negativity has this brought upon people and the world? Thoughts are part of the ego. There is a balanced ego and an unbalanced ego. A balanced ego is the part of you that identifies what you like and what you don't like. A balanced ego is connected to your personality and how you view the world. An unbalanced ego is thinking that everything is all about you, that only your thoughts and desires matter, that you are right and everyone else is wrong, and nothing else is important to you besides your wants and desires. We want to live with the balanced ego. Ego is good. There is no need to destroy it, rather you can make it the way you want it to be. Again, you are in control and create your reality in all ways. Ego help us live and enjoy the pleasures of life. Combine ego with compassion and love and you are good to go. Again, it's part of the practice. The thoughts and unbalanced ego are like a newborn baby. It wants your constant attention. I know most of you have commitments, bills, families, friends, problems, jobs, goals, and so on. Now that is a lot to think about, right? I agree. But, there is a way to have all that in your life and still be in the present moment, with little-to-no thought.

It is possible to use the thinking process only when it's needed to do whatever is necessary for the present moment. Whether you need to pay your bills, or you want to create something. Be fully present in the moment. Think about a single point, right now. Being fully immersed in whatever you are doing, moment to moment, is being in "the Now." As long as you are awake, you are always doing something. Most people are busy doing something in the moment while thinking about a thousand other things. You are currently reading this book right now, but occasionally may think of something else: what to eat for dinner, a conversation you had earlier, what is going to happen tomorrow, what's that feeling in my body, does he or she like me, should I be doing something else right now, and so on. Thinking never ends. You could sit in one spot all day and never stop thinking. Doctors call this "Attention Deficit Disorder," thinking one thing and then another, and another, and another. This is also known as the "monkey mind." The mind just keeps going and going, thought after thought after thought. Thoughts are partly just bits of recycled data, such as thoughts or situations that happened in the past. They also make up our imagination. Both thoughts and imagination exist in the realm of time and space, but not in the now. When you resort to a default mode of thinking or unconsciously using your imagination, you take yourself out of the present moment, where everything you desire and want to feel lives. On the flipside, if you deliberately use your thoughts and imagination to create what you want, you are now working with the tools of the balanced ego and positive thinking. This is a powerful mental antidote to successfully achieve whatever you want.

Every thought has an energy force that wants to pull you into action. "Oh, look at this! Let me think about that. What's that? Who is this? What should I eat? Shouldn't I be doing something else? I don't like that. I like that. Oh look, a text message. Look at this email. A app notification. Oh, I want to read this. Should I call this person? Why did that happen yesterday? What if this happens tomorrow? What if this gets me? What if I don't get this? Am I doing this correctly? Am I good enough? What does this person think of me? What do I think of that person?" These are all just thoughts, they are not who you are. People can spend their days possessed by thought. They live their entire lives chasing thoughts. The media industry has capitalized on the monkey mind, especially television. Have you ever watched a commercial or T.V show and noticed how quick the images on the screen come and go? They know that your attention span is very short. "Watch this. Buy this. Go here. Go there. Consume and spend all your money! You're not good enough as you are. You need to be better!" Whoa, what a mess!

Now what I am suggesting is to take time out of your day to go inside, (details on this later) be still, and realize the Source energy within your body that will keep you entertained for all of eternity! Have you ever said to yourself: "I can't do this anymore," or "I can't live this way," or "I can't live with myself!" Who is the "I" in these statements? The "I" is the Source energy within you that wants your attention directed to the aliveness of your inner body, the beauty of nature, the positive feeling of bliss when you live out your dreams and passion! This is who you really are and what you can pay attention to. Not just your thoughts, or your memories, or your ego, or your body, or your senses and desires, or your Facebook news feed! As humans, we excel at creating something in our minds, something that may not even be true or part of our existence, and then convince ourselves that it is true or that it did or might happen. Now this is what you want to do if you intend to use the Law of Attraction for positive creation. Creating a story in your mind of something you want to experience in the future, is to use your powerful imagination in a productive and positive way as part of your creation process. Remember, the first evidence of physical manifestation is the emotional feeling

34

arising inside your gut and heart, which blossomed from your intentional use of imagination. Most people use this power to focus on unwanted things and negative emotions, or relive negative past experiences. Do you see the silliness of this? People think about something over and over again until they trick themselves into believing it is true. Even if it was true when it happened, it may not still be true in the present moment. This creates fear and worry. You think something negative, identify with it and make it into a reality, when really it could be the furthest thing from your current reality. Feeling negative emotion is the first indicator that you are creating something unwanted. I know you know someone that lives this way and has shared this with you. Or it might even be you! And that's fine! The first step is being mindful enough to realize what you are thinking about and doing in that moment. You can then stop yourself in the act before Law of Attraction gets ahold of it. So good! The lesson here is to do your best to deliberately focus on thoughts that make you feel good. Only think and talk about what you want to create. It can be that simple.

If you can see your thoughts as just thoughts and nothing more, you will begin to intuitively know which thoughts to pay attention to and which ones are just filling up space. You learn to ignore most of your random thoughts that don't feel good. If a kid is not interested in something you are doing, what do they do? Ignore you! You learn how to do the same thing with most of your thoughts. Eventually, all the random or negative thoughts start to disappear because you don't pay attention to them anymore. They lose power when you stop taking them so seriously. You literally just stop caring. You stop identifying who you are with thought. In this state, when you do have a thought you will feel it intuitively. You then feel the rightness and goodness of that thought and don't question it because you know it will benefit a present or future situation you may be dealing with. You now begin to use thought to assist you in whatever you are doing in your Now. This is a healthy mind. If you are fully present in your Now and a thought impulse lights up your whole body with joy and excitement, that is the thought to pay attention to, act on, plan on, or do whatever feels right in that moment. You can trust this. Use thought to get more specific on things that feel good to you, or to create something new. If you're in a state of bliss, and a thought comes that makes you feel better, listen and follow that thought. You have to retrain yourself how to think, my friends. It takes practice, and help from someone who has already done this work. (More on finding a teacher later on!)

Use thought as a tool to live moment to moment, instead of allowing them to rule your life. When you are feeling good, thought will assist you with whatever you want to do or create. It is a tool to live a happy life, not dwell on the past or what might happen in the future. Thinking this way brings up so much regret and fear in humans. You don't want to feel that, do you? Fear and regret? No! You want to feel good! So chill out and be easy about this. Practice watching your mind and learn how it works. Then master your mind. Pretend your thoughts are a horse and you, Source energy in a body, are the rider. You choose the direction you want the horse to go. You love and respect the horse, for it is part of you. But you are in control, not the horse. Similarly, you can be in control of your thoughts, rather than your thoughts being in control of you!

: PART II :

Now that you understand who you really are, that the now moment is the only moment there is, and how your mind and the Law Of Attraction work, it's time to do your part of the work! In the chapters to come, you will learn to dive deep into the depths of your soul and find the doors where you locked up and threw away the key. We will find those keys and shine light upon the issues, trauma, and pain that you may have suppressed and hidden from yourself and others. I also will talk about drugs and addiction, why people get sick and depressed, and how to protect yourself from unwanted energy and situations. Lastly, I discuss the "what about me" trip. You're going to dig all this! Get excited! It's going to be a wild ride! Don't be scared now, I will hold your hand the entire time. Take a deep breath, and let's go!

: 4 :

REALIZING & DOING YOUR DEEP DARK WORK

If you're always thinking about the past or the future, you are never fully present in the Now. As I write this, I think about what I'm doing now, not about what I'm saying. What I am experiencing is not really thinking at all actually. The words are just flowing through me. There is not much thought happening in my mind. I'm not thinking about what I did earlier, nor my friend sitting across from me, nor what happened to me in the past or what might happen to me in the future. I am purely in the moment. No thought is required to be in the moment. It's a letting go of control and just being with what is. Just being with what is. Surrendering yourself to the moment as it is, without the need to change anything. Most people are always wanting to fix, control, and figure every little thing out. When you do this, you leave the present moment and go into thought, which is involved with time. Being in the Now is timeless. It takes courage and practice to live in the Now, with mindfulness, peace, and pure love in your heart. It requires focus and attention to what is going on in your mind and body. You go from focusing mainly on the external world and chasing your thoughts, to focusing on your inner world and outer world equally. Mindful focus allows your mind and body to thrive with joy in its natural human state.

It is understandably difficult to stop yourself from constantly focusing on past negativity and trauma, or to disassociate with past or present thoughts, emotions, and memories. When you become still and quiet your mind, all those past and present images, negative emotions, and feelings come up to torment you. As a result, many people ignore the present moment and get busy with external stuff, internal stress, and gossip. I have been in that headspace also. When I was first learning to meditate, I experienced unwanted and negative emotions, thoughts, or physical pain on a regular basis. As I became still and quiet, while walking in nature for instance, my thoughts slowed down. Then all the negative stuff that I carried in this life and past lives came up in that moment of stillness and silence. They took me out of the moment into negative emotion. These feelings, images, thoughts, or pains arose because they wanted to be realized, healed, and released from my body, mind, and soul. Think of these negative emotions and feelings like a young hurt child wanting relief, who needs our attention to be nurtured and healed. I am here to tell you it is possible to overcome your pain, negative thoughts, emotions, and past traumatizing experiences no matter what they are. It is possible to have ease and comfort in your mind and body right now, in this moment.

Acceptance is an important part of the healing process. If you find yourself constantly fighting against thoughts or a situation, then you will remain stuck in it. If you can let life unfold without completely identifying with what happens around you and within your mind, then you will find peace and ease. From this feeling of peace and ease, you become present in the Now and feel good. I am not saying you shouldn't care about life, your relationships, your past, or to not have preferences, opinions, and beliefs. I'm saying that it's up to you to determine how you let the past or present unfolding of your life affect you. How much do you attach who you are as a human to what happened in the past, or fear what might happen in the future? It's your choice. You can still care deeply about an event or someone, and at the same time not let it corrupt the core essence of who you are inside. Not allow it to become an obsessive thought, or control your life and mood. There has to be a surrendering to what is. You must let go of what holds you back from being all that you are meant to be in this lifetime. Release and heal your past, and trust in what is to come. And you do all this by understanding how the universe works and that you create your own reality. By also understanding that when you feel good, you create ease and joy in your present moment and all the moments to come!

If the thought you are thinking now does not feel good emotionally, then that is your guidance system telling you to stop paying attention to that thought, or rethink it in a way that does feels better. Even if it's true. Even if it is real life, or it's about the past, present, or future. It doesn't matter. If the thought you are thinking does not feel good, that feeling is your guidance system within you telling you those thoughts are not in alignment with who you are and what Source knows to be true about you. Your emotions are the guidance system that lets you know moment-to-moment, thought-by-thought, what thoughts to pay attention to and what thoughts to ignore. This guidance is always there and will never steer you wrong, I promise you this. When you think a thought that feels bad it is either not true, or it's a distorted way of thinking that does not serve you at all. Now if the thought you are thinking feels good, that is your guidance system saying "Yes! That's the right path. Do and think more of that!" If you're thinking something and it doesn't feel good, why keep thinking about it? To figure it out? Why force something to happen using thought or action? The best times in life happen with ease, grace, and little-to-no effort.

Think about the best, most exciting trips and events in your life, and how they manifested. You see, you can never stop thought. It's impossible. So when you think a thought that doesn't feel so good emotionally, try to change your approach and your attitude. Think the thought in a way that feels good, or change the subject all together so that it does feel good. Make it the story of how you want it to be, even if it's made up. When you do this you make the present moment your friend, and not your enemy. Your thoughts create your emotions, and your emotions create your reality. What you feel, you get. The content of your thoughts are past memories, either real or imagined. If your thoughts cause you suffering, then you are suffering from something that does not exist. I say again, thoughts are just repetitive past information or imagination. Human thought is meant to be used as a tool to manage and create your life. Thoughts are not life itself. Life does not live in your brain. Life happens within the wholeness of who you are as a conscious being. Reflect on that for a moment and take some deep, soft breaths.

I am illustrating the process of listening to your guidance system because it is an important tool for living happily. It is so important for understanding why things happen to you, and how wanted and unwanted things come to you. It's not a big mystery anymore, my friends. This is truly how everything works. I have been practicing this for years. I, and many others, are living proof that these teachings really work if you practice them! I bring it up in this section of the book because when your body and mind become silent and still, but negative thoughts, images, words, or life experiences come to mind anyway, it is your soul's way of telling you to pay attention to it, to heal it, and release it. Not to continue ignoring it. If the negative emotion, thought, or feeling comes up day after day, it wants your attention for a reason. It wants to be healed and released from your energy and soul. If the same negativity is continuously replaying while you sit in daily meditation or enjoy nature, that time someone abused you, a story of something which triggers negative emotions, or even a single word which causes that negative emotion, then you need to pay attention and do the work to release it. For if you don't they will never fully go away.

There was a time when a word would constantly come into my mind when I was still and silent. I did my work on it, and it went away. The work I did on this subject was massive and powerful and changed my life experience entirely. So, sometimes just ignoring the thoughts and stories that don't feel good to us is not enough. Most of the time when something is repeatedly triggering negative emotions, it means you need to observe it, respond to it, and allow it to be. This negative emotion can be stress, fear, worry, guilt, doubt, physical pain, or even anxiety and panic attacks. You are not supposed to feel those things. So if you do, take a deep breath, relax, and know that there is a way to release what is bothering you and holding you back from living the most beautiful, ease-filled, and loving life you could ever imagine. Do your work and all is coming.

: CREATE HEALING & FREEDOM BY DOING YOUR DEEP DARK WORK :

When you feel negative emotion in your body, or keep thinking a specific negative thought that won't go away, this is your soul saying that there is something deeper here than just thought and physical pain that needs to be clearly observed, healed, and set free. It is time to put the microscope right on the core issue at hand. Time to find the hidden key and open the darkest, most painful doors of your soul. Often we need help from another to locate that key, find the doors, and do the healing work. Everyone has work to do: Jesus, Buddha, Oprah, me, everyone! For some it may be a little, for some it may be a lot. It all depends on how much work you have done in your current life and in past lives. All of us need to do what I call the "deep dark work!" So many people ignore this work. People go lifetimes ignoring this work. I call it "deep dark work" because it is emotions, thoughts, and current life or past life events that are stuck deep down in our bodies. These things hide in the darkest dungeons of our souls, away from yourself and everyone else.

No light shines where this pain and suffering lives. We need to go down to the dungeon and shine the Divine light of healing, for when that healing lights shines down there it never ceases. When we first begin this deep dark work a great fear may possibly overcome us. We go down to the door, see it clearly and panic, or go into shock and run away. We go back to our smartphones and our busy lives with all of our friends who are also hiding and afraid of their deep dark work, and rightfully so.

This chapter is all about doing your deep dark work! Get excited! It doesn't matter how old you are, what state your body and mind is in, how bad you think you got it, how much you were abused and destroyed, or how horrible of a person you think you are. It doesn't matter. You can heal, grow, and experience love and bliss right now in this lifetime! This is your birthright. Don't skip ahead, because this is one of the most powerful chapters in this book! After much of this work is done, life starts to get really awesome and fun, even more than it is now! Darkness turns into light. Anxiety turns into ease and comfort. Pain turns into pleasure. Fear turns into love. I promise you this, brothers and sisters. But it only happens when you locate and open the hidden door with the key. The key is shining your healing light of love on the wounds that stifle your potential and prevent you from attaining ultimate freedom, joy, peace of mind, and love.

Another important thing to realize is this: You are not broken. You are not defective. You're not a bad person, and there is nothing wrong with you. Don't compare your deep dark work with anyone else's. This is all part of your journey here on Earth. If you have emotional or physical pain, negative thoughts that won't go away, dreams or images that trouble you, anxiety, depression, sadness, anything negative that doesn't feel good and that won't go away, then you have to pay attention and work on it. And you have to do it now. If it is coming up in your awareness that means the time to do the work is now, not in a couple years, not after you try the medication and talk to the doctor or therapist. Now. If you don't do your work now, it will remain stuck in this lifetime and in every other life you choose to live. This work might be scary at first, and that is why at first most of us need help from another to heal. Find somebody you trust and love 110 percent. It can be someone with credentials in a specific field of study, such as an energy focused therapist, or an energy healer, guru, shaman, a family member or best friend. But, the helper you choose must be willing and able to ride the deep dark wave with you all the way. They must be able to help you find the true reason for your suffering and assist you in releasing the unwanted energy from your body and mind completely. Just plain talking to someone does not do it. I'm sorry, words don't truly heal. The healer you choose has to be able to understand what you are going through, help you find the core of the issue and see it clearly, and assist you in releasing the unwanted energy, memory, attachment, person, entity, and so on. They must be trained or have a solid method to assist you in recognizing the unwanted issues, learn from them, heal and release them completely from your energetic soul body. I call it "soul surgery." Whichever healer you choose, they must have experience with what you want to do. And what you want to do is to go to the core of the issue. The core of the negative emotion or thought. The core of the image or word, the core of the story, the core of the pain, the core of the dream, the core of the experience. You have to open the door labeled "deep dark work." Open it, walk down the stairs all the way and shine your light completely on the heart of the matter. You have to go all the way. Go only part way, you only get healed part way. It may be very intense work, but have no fear. This too shall pass, and it will pass quickly if you completely release what wants to be healed. This healing process may be fast, it may be slow. It all depends on what you are ready to release and allow. How much are you willing to give up and how much are you ready to attain?

Your assistant or healer will come to you when you are ready and sincere about doing your deep dark work. And when you meet them you will know they are your healer. All my gurus, healers, and helpers came to me effortlessly. Once you find them, give yourself completely to this person. You must surrender and be able to have complete trust and love in this person. Trust and love is the main ingredient here. You have to feel comfortable fully sharing your deep dark work with them. You can't be afraid to open up to this person, for this is the only way to heal and let go of your unwanted. Dive deep into the underworld of your heart, mind, and soul. There lies the coiled serpent snake named "Kundalini," the energetic snake coiled up at the base of your spine in your root chakra. There lies your deepest darkest pains and secrets, all your deep dark work or what you might call your deepest issues, problems, and fears. All the negative things you did in a past life or this one. By doing your work you release the fear and free the serpent from its cage. The Kundalini snake holds all the love, power, and healing you are seeking. Do your work, and the snake hurls out of its cage of fear and moves into the blissful state of love and light in your heart.

I was so afraid to do my deep dark work and awaken my snake. To look into his eyes and see the truth, everything I was suppressing and hiding away. Engaging in your deep dark work takes courage, trust, and true faith in your healer and in Source. But let me tell you this right now, my friend: it is possible and worth it! If something keeps coming up which prevents you from realizing your potential, then take the time to see it clearly and heal it. I'm going to keep reminding you throughout the book that you have to make this life experience extremely personal and customize it to who you are and what you want. Don't compare your life or experience to anyone else's, especially their spiritual practices, healing, deep dark work, or the unfolding of their life. We will always have something that needs to be worked on, healed, and let go. It becomes less intense and influential on your well-being the more work you do. After some time this work just becomes fun daily maintenance. You can try to do your deep dark work alone, like the Buddha did underneath the bodhi tree through deep intense meditation, self realization, and surrender to the powerful intentions he set. But living in this age with all its modern-day distractions, it is very difficult - possible - but difficult to take that path. Most of us need the help of another healer or master. Someone who has gone through what you are going through now and has done their own deep dark work. I can not stress this enough. Don't be afraid to ask for help. If you feel you need it, you're right. There is no shame. No blame. No right or wrong here. Listen to your body, listen to your heart. Go deep into the abyss of your mind and soul, because from there you find the light of love and ease you never thought was possible. That light is pure Source energy. Pure light love energy is waiting for you to realize it and use it to create whatever you want in this lifetime.

Get rid of everything and everyone that is holding you back. Only you know what and who that is. Until you do this deep dark soul work, it will be very hard for you to be in the present moment for any extended period of time. For when you meditate and become present, the deep dark work will show its face to you and do whatever it needs to get your attention. Meditation is a wonderful tool to realize what work needs to be done. When your mind becomes still and silent, you clearly see your thoughts and life, all the good and bad. This is a gift. To see clearly is one of the greatest gifts of all. Realize this work and rejoice because now you know what must be done! And after the work is done the next version of you will be more blissful than you could even imagine. But ignore the work and it will just come back. So why not get it over with? It's quite fun, and not as scary as you think it is. So chill out, take a few deep breaths and get on with it. It will all be okay, I promise. It might be intense and scary while you are doing the work, but it is only temporary and nothing but ease, fun, bliss, joy, and love is waiting for you at the other end. Be open to finding your healer, tell them what is going on, do the process of healing that feels right for you, and do it fully. Your body will let you know who you need, what you need, and how to to heal. Trust your gut and you heart. The more you open yourself up to this person and surrender yourself to the healing process, the quicker the healing and relief will come. If you only give a little, you get a little. Go in halfway, you get only half. Get it? Go all the way, and go now.

Some people might not need this intense deep work. Maybe you did it in your past lives. Your childhood and present life might have been awesome and mostly positive. Mine has been. I personally had to do a lot of intense past life work. Little things of course came up here and there when I was a kid. For instance, I had abandonment issues when I was very young. My loving parents observed this and helped me to do my deep dark work to heal the issue with quickness and ease. I know these teachings to be true for me, because when I do my work and let it go without over thinking or trying to figure it out, I feel like a brand new human. I feel like I have a brand new body and mind. I am still Mahkah, just version 9.0. It's like installing an update on your phone or computer. After installation is complete it's still the same device or app, just better, more enjoyable, more effective, and more fun!

Once the majority of your work is done, it is much simpler to live in the Now and enjoy life. Your work might not need to be deep intense reflection and bringing up past wounds. It might just be accepting the past, and moving on, and not thinking about all those things that make you feel uncomfortable. But, if your body hurts, or your mind keeps thinking about things that happened, or an image or word is bothering you, then you have to pay attention to it and do your work. Have no fear. The work you do benefits not only you, but everyone around you. You're doing so well, and things from this point forward will only become clearer and more exciting for you. There is work to be done, my friend.

Do it knowing that "this too shall pass." Magical clarity and love is waiting for you on the other side, dwelling in the present moment. You are a powerful warrior of love; nothing can stand in your way now. Knowledge is power. Everything you need to do your work you already have. Do it on your own, or find another to assist you in this process of healing and growth! You got this and I believe in you!

: 5 :

DRUGS & ADDICTION

When you are suffering, and have not developed a consistent spiritual practice of some kind, are not aware of the Now and the Law Of Attraction, haven't done your deep dark work, and don't know that you have Source power within you, then it is easy to look to external things to make you healthy, whole, and happy. There are many pleasurable things out there which please the senses, such as drugs. People find stuff they enjoy, feel pleasure from it, and use it to make them feel alive and free because they think that they can't feel good without it. Or they have something going on inside their mind or body that they don't know how to handle and need a way to not feel or think about it. People want relief. People want to feel good. You intuitively know that you are meant to feel amazing in this moment! When you don't, you feel really bad and want it to change, and change quickly. People think the only option is an external way, when the real way is internal. This is how addictions manifest. We are all creatures of habit. Everyone I know is addicted to something, whether it be substance addiction like drugs, caffeine, cannabis, alcohol, or process and behavioral addictions such as food, shopping, games, Netflix, sex, exercise, or thinking. Yes, thinking. It can be anything. What is the true reason behind why we become addicted to something? One can say it is to relieve a mental or physical feeling or emotion, to numb our body and minds. We want to forget the mental or physical pain stemming from whatever is happening now or what happened in the past. When we don't do our deep dark work, when we suppress our negative emotions and our feelings, we feel the need to cover them up. Most people don't know there are options besides drugs. When we don't do that deep dark soul work I explained in the previous chapter, it becomes almost impossible sometimes to live. So we mask, we cover up, we coat it. To do so does nothing but hide it. It's a temporary cover to forget about whatever it is that is bothering you. Whatever is hiding in the shadows is begging to come out.

In the long run, drugs and other addictions only end up intensifying whatever you are hiding from, causing these things to rise more dramatically to the surface. For example, have you ever had a friend who would drink too much alcohol and turn into a completely different person? Maybe they would become mean, aggressive, disrespectful, or very depressed? I think people call alcohol a "depressant" because it brings up the darkness within us. The deep dark work shows its face. It says, "Hello! I'm in here, and I want to come out and heal! Pay attention to me! It's going to be so much better when I'm gone!" Nobody wants to feel bad. We all intuitively know that we came into this life to feel good and have fun. Because you know you are here to feel good and have fun, when you don't you then look to external things instead of doing your deep soul work. People chase more money, more houses, more relationships, more food, more vacations, more cars, more sex, more stuff, it never ends. These are all wonderful to have when we want them from a place of pure enjoyment. But so many are using these external things to fill them up, to make themselves happy and whole. The saying goes: "Money doesn't buy happiness." The happiness and fulfillment you seek externally must first be found internally. From that place of internal fulfillment and wholeness, you will feel more amazing than you ever thought you could feel when you do seek external pleasures.

Before I continue, it's important to mention the number one, most powerful addiction: thinking. Yes, thought. We are obsessed with it. Some people go their entire lives chasing their thoughts when they are not sleeping. Chasing thoughts this way and that way. All around. Chapter Three is devoted to explaining how the mind works, so I won't go into it again. I bring it up here so you will keep in mind the power thought has to take you out of the Now, to create worry, stress, and thought-induced suffering. In Part Three, I cover meditation and mindfulness, which become very powerful and effective tools in dealing with the mind's antics.

So back to the drugs, yeah? One reason for drug-use is to mask the negative emotions or situations people don't want to deal with. Not all of us do, however. I know enlightened people who enjoy herb, wine, and hallucinogens here and there. It's all about balance and what works for you. Besides hiding from, ignoring, and covering up our deep dark work, why would we really do any type of drug? A second reason we turn to drugs is to make the Now experience something more than what it naturally is. We are all experience seekers. When you unconsciously take drugs, you are trying to change something from what it is to what you wish it was. You want your present reality to be better than it is because it is unpleasing in some way. This is not a bad way to look at life, but it is possible to achieve this desire without drugs. Drugs change your current moment very quickly, and can give you that feeling of no thought, of flowing in the moment with Source. You might use the drug to feel certain things that may not be possible to feel on your own. Some people say they live such boring, mundane, and unenjoyable lives, so they use drugs to experience a sense of relief or pleasure. Say you have a job that you can't stand, for example. When work is done for the day you come home and have a toke or a beer to experience something else, to forget about the stress of your day-to-day life. You are unhappy with your current life, so you use whatever drug or substance to make you feel at ease and relaxed. Many people live this way. Yes, what you feel while taking the substance is relief, and you may forget about your stresses for a moment or two. But this it is still just coating, masking, and covering it up. Nothing changes after the high wears off. No work gets done internally or externally. It's the lazy way of changing your life. And it's not changing your life, it's just altering the current moment for a short period of time.

When you're high, you are not fully you anymore. Your body and mind are reacting to something to you put in it, which only brings you into a state or numbness and ease. Sooner or later it goes away, and you want more. Herein lies the addiction. People think they can't feel this way on their own, so they chase the high. This is probably why they call it getting high. When intoxicated you might think you feel high, flying with Source energy because you forget about your problems and all the things you wish were different about your life. Yes, the feeling is real because you are experiencing it. But the feeling you seek from taking the drug goes away, and then come the side effects. There is a reason why you feel like crap the next day if you drink too much alcohol.

Our society has declared hangovers and prescription drugs to be a normal part of human life. Feel depressed? There's a pill for that. Feel tired? There's a pill for that. Want to lose some weight? There's a pill for that. Can't sleep at night? There's a pill for that, too. Have you seen the prescription drug advertisements on television where they talk about what the drug does for 15 seconds, and then talk about all the drug's side effects for another 1 minute or so? It's ironic that people who feel so much pain and hopelessness are willing to risk their lives to ease a headache, balance their cholesterol, or alleviate depression and sadness. We forget how powerful we are. What if I told you that you can feel higher than you ever thought possible, without the drugs? To be intoxicated in your body and your mind completely clear? This is possible, friends! This is what you really want from the drugs. To be blissed out, healthy and pain-free in your body, and completely clear and easy in your mind. I feel this right now as I am writing. My body is intoxicated and high as can be, but I am clear and focused in my mind. Others have stated that they feel this same way without drugs. You are reaching for an experience of ease and oneness with Source. This is a connection of body, mind, and spirit in union with Source energy in the present moment.

Let me be clear now. I'm not saying that all substances and drugs are negative and should never be used. Some substances can be used as tools to find awakening and alignment with Source energy. Substances that come straight from Mother Earth, cannabis, mushrooms, peyote, and ayahuasca for instance, can be used as tools for awakening, healing, creating art, and connecting deeply with nature, other people, and the Divine Mother. Some indigenous peoples have been using plants and herbs for healing and transformation since the beginning of time. Some substances and plants are very powerful tools when used in an intentional way for healing, growth, and creation. Some people use these substances to heal deep emotional wounds and addictions, to assist in gaining clarity and insight into their lives, and to realize who they are and why they are here. This process of self-exploration can also happen during meditation. As I stated before, some of us need help to reach enlightenment. Some people need the teacher/guru path. For some, the drug is the guru. Some people need the yogic asana and meditation path. Others need to have an experience with a shaman and a substance to heal and open up their doors. Again, you must personalize your path. I am not saying go to an electronic music festival and take entheogen with your friends to heal your deep dark work. I am saying that taking a substance in a spiritual and mindful way, with guidance from a shaman or elder in a ceremonial setting with the intention to heal, transform, and grow, can be a very powerful tool. Of course, I only advocate a guided drug experience if it is allowed by local laws. I do not advocate breaking any laws or regulations to do this work.

Substances and entheogens intentionally used in a mindful, and legal, way can be very powerful healing tools to help us awaken, heal deep dark work, connect deeply to people, nature, our passions, and even help find our path to enlightenment. It is similar to how the path of yoga can be used as a tool. Cannabis is now being used as a means to treat horrible, chronic pain. What a gift! Some people have neurochemical imbalances and they need a substance or drug in order to function in the world. I am all for this. Again, it comes down to intention and balance. In some cases, substances can be helpful, but once you commit to a spiritual path, open the doors, and turn on the light, then you may no longer desire to partake in them. We are experience seekers, and want more things that feel good. Once our work is done, we can use our alignment with Source energy in the Now to get high without using the substances. Once you do your deep dark work, and the light is on, you get high from life. It is the high that comes from the natural energy of being fully alive, healthy, and conscious in a human body! This is a scientific fact! Once the light is on, it never goes out. The light of clarity and pure alignment with Source energy is more powerful than any other drug or substance on this planet.

I do believe that if we align with Source energy unconditionally through our bodies, senses, and intentions, we alone have the power to bring our bodies and minds back into balance to heal and grow. We have the power to do whatever we believe. We can grow back limbs if we truly believed we could. We can get back our lost vision or hearing if we truly believed it in every cell of our bodies! But governments and media want us to think we are not the powerful beings that deep down we know we are. Hollywood movies trick us into believing we are not powerful creators, and we say things like, "That only happens in the movies." Other people declare this is real, or that is not real. "Oh, that only happens in fairytales! Humans are only capable of doing this, and not that. Only superheroes, witches, and fictional characters can do theses things." No! The power that creates worlds resides within us all, people! We can do, be, or have anything we want! We just have to identify what we want, believe it to be true unconditionally, and get out of our own way. You are a powerful creator! You are that which you call "God" in a physical body! The Earth also provides us with whatever we want and need to experience. So listen to your body, listen to your impulses from that place of feeling good, and do what you need to do. Many paths all lead to the same place. That place is pure bliss, joy, and clarity, and it is possible for every human to reach and experience it.

If you choose to use a substances to assist your healing and growing process, please do so mindfully, legally, and with intention. You have to make this spiritual path personal. Substances that come from the Earth are here for a reason. They help some of us find a place of truth, center, balance, and awakening in our bodies, hearts, and minds. Listen to you body, it will tell you what it needs. When you trust your guides and your gut, you are really just trusting yourself.

: 6 :

SICKNESS & DEPRESSION

When you have no mindful connection to nature, no control over your body's emotions and energies, including awareness of Source energy within you, then you can become physically or mentally sick. This is to say that something is off-balance or needs to be released from your body or thought process. What I understand about sickness or depression is that it usually caused by one of two things. The first is that you have identified with something outside of yourself, outside of your body and mind's energy and vibration. You have identified who you are with something that is not you at all. For example, identification with a role as a wife or a father, or you have identified your existence based on how much money you make or how many possessions you have. Or you identify your existence based on what your friends, family, social peers, or lover think about you. If you identify who you are with something that is not inside of you, something that is not you, and you become attached to this identity, role or method, then you will become disappointed and let down when the attachment does not bring you the happiness or joy that you thought it would. People want external things because they believe having them will relieve their suffering or bring happiness. The belief that external things bring happiness and fulfillment is a false one. You try to accumulate more stuff or relationships in order to lessen stress and create happiness. In doing so you create more bills, more responsibilities, more relationships. You lose sight of who you really are and why you have come. You become so anxious and stressed out trying to maintain your busy life and all the people in it, that your body eventually freaks out and you develop an addiction, get stressed out, or become sick or depressed. It's a mess. People are constantly using other people and things to make them happy and whole. To make them feel worthy. People use things outside of their body to try to heal their deep dark work. It will never work. As I went over in Chapter Four, only going inside is the true path to healing and growth. This all comes down to balance. Have friends, buy stuff, take out loans, but do so in a mindful way. Being mindful means to clearly see the reason why you are doing something. You can have a spiritual practice, run a business, have nice things, and be in perfect health and healing all at the same time.

Now the second cause of sickness and depression is the identification with, and attachment to, mind-made negative thought patterns and beliefs that continuously dominate your thoughts and keep you stuck in negative emotions. You become obsessed with those negative thoughts. You can become addicted to those negative thoughts. Negative thoughts make you feel bad, so the Law of Attraction keeps bringing you more and more of the same because that is how you are feeling. Your thoughts are very powerful because they create your reality. What you think about the most, you get. That is why it is important to be aware of your thoughts and know which ones to focus on and which ones to ignore. You know this by the way the thought makes you feel emotionally. When you think negative thoughts all the time, or even a little bit, you start to feel really horrible. After a time you lose or forget about your connection to the God within you. The God within you knows that you want to feel alive and happy and worthy, so when you think otherwise you feel great internal discord. Over time you keep feeding and riding this chain of pain and the universe shows you more and more things to feel bad about. You feel worse and worse until someone looks at you and labels you "depressed," which by the way is just a word humans made up. Words alone have no power. It's the feeling and emotion behind the word that creates your reality. We are all masters, and yet we are skilled in training ourselves to feel the opposite of what you and the God within know to be true. The Law of Attraction will bring you more of what you are feeling, whether it is wanted or unwanted, and thoughts create those feelings. This negative thinking and feeling can go on for months or even years, until one day you can't take life any more and you want to check out. If something unwanted happens to you, it is labeled as "bad" or "negative." You then try to figure out why it happened, and how to not let it happen again. By doing this you give your attention to the thing you don't want to have happen or think about. By giving your attention to the subject and thought that is making you feel bad you keep it vibrating in your system and you keep feeling bad, even though your intention is to make it go away and feel good. You give the negative emotion power by trying to make it go away. We use past events to justify our lives and give meaning to who we are. We say things like, "This happened to me so that is why I feel like this." Or, "This person did this to me so that is why I feel like this." You lose your self-worth and power over something that happened to you in the past. You forget that you are a strong and powerful creator! You lose your power when you let negative thoughts of past experiences dictate your Now! By focusing on the unwanted and keeping that vibration in your body, you are watering the plant. You need to water a different plant. The plant of what you do want and how you do want to feel. Do you get this? This is big. Whatever you habitually focus on, the universe gives you more of it. Mic drop.

What to do? You want to focus as best as you can on what you do want, which is to feel good. When you are in a state of mostly feeling good, the universe will give you everything that you declared you ever wanted, from every life you have ever lived, unfolding in perfect time. Simply put, feeling good brings about more good in every area of your life. It waters the plant that produces more fruit to feel good about. Feeling bad brings more bad to the matters you care about, and waters the plant that feeds your reasons to feel bad. I bring up the Law of Attraction throughout the book because this is how everything works. Creation depends upon your emotions. Emotions are your powerful, personal guidance system. All of us have this guidance system, and it will never leave you or misguide you. Your understanding of the system or its guidance can be distorted, but it will never mislead you. If you focus on the bad to try and feel good, you're still focusing on the bad. Feel good! If thinking about something makes you feel bad, stop it! You think it's normal to always have stress in your life. You think it's normal to always have a problem that needs fixing. You think it's normal to always be worrying about something. You think this is all normal life on planet Earth. It's not! It is the complete opposite. Just because so many people are depressed and stressed out, doesn't mean it's how things have to be! You are Source; pure, positive energy in a body! You intended this to be a remarkable experience! Sure, there will be a few bumps in the road, or a lot at times. But focus on the joy of the ride itself, not the bumps. The bumps create contrast to help you focus on what you do want, by knowing what you don't want. Give your attention to the solution, not the problem. The problems create the solutions. In the problem lives the solution. You cannot have one without the other. Negative things will surely happen from time to time. What's more important is how you internally handle the negative thoughts and situations as they arise, rather than how they are dealt with externally. If you truly believe that things are always working out for you, which is universal truth for all humans, then applying these teachings to your life will be much easier than you think. This life is supposed to be fun, fun, fun! So get on with it!

Depression occurs when you hold onto negative thoughts and past experiences long enough that the universe aligns with this vibration and brings about more things to feel bad about. Focus on negative, you get more negative. You lose your job, then your car breaks down, then you get sick, you get into an accident, and so on and so forth. It does not end until you change your focus and way of thinking. Yes, you! Nobody can do this for you. No pill or doctor can do it for you. People and substances may help a bit, but you've got to find it within yourself to bring positive attention to what you want. This may be hard to hear if you are deep in a hole. Believe me when I say I have been in that same hole, my friend. But there is help out there. There are ladders and ropes that will help you rise to the surface, to ease, comfort and love. And now you know how to get out of this hole. If you need help don't be ashamed to ask for it. But just know that you have the power to do this on your own. All you have to do is try a little bit of what I am suggesting, and watch how you feel. Mindful, deliberate actions of wanting to feel good will gracefully bring to you out of this hole. Part III of this book will offer you tools to implement these teachings into your everyday life in a simple, yet powerful way. I'm not bashing the seriousness of depression, and if you have lost someone you love because of it, I am truly sorry. My intention is to help you understand why and how it happens to most people, and how to heal and release it based on my own experiences and what I have learned from people close to me.

What do you to do if you or a loved one is feeling down or depressed? Step one is to fully accept what is and trust that you can change. This might be the hardest part. Accept that this is your current state, but let go of fear because your current state is constantly changing and evolving every second. When someone is deep in a hole, it can be a slow process to get them out, depending on how deep the hole is. Abraham Hicks gives a great example of a speeding train going 100 miles per hour in one direction; you don't want the train to immediately turn around and go the other direction, do you? It will destroy the train and everyone onboard. It has to be a slow turnaround. Baby steps. How long the process takes depends on the person and the situation. For example, you can go from a state of despair to a state of depression. From depression to a state of rage.

From rage to anger. From anger to sadness. From sadness to exhaustion. From exhaustion to fear. From fear to hope. From hope to trust. From trust to knowing. From knowing to love. From love to compassion. And so on. Step two is to focus your attention on anything in the world that feels good. Don't try to put a positive spin on the stuff that does not feel good. Focus on something else, anything else that easily brings a smile to your face and the light of love into your body. Watch your favorite movie. Eat your favorite food. Go dancing. Listen to your favorite music. Ride your bike. Hang out with people that love you. Read a good book. Go on vacation. Lay in the sun and pet your dog. Do anything to feel good! Anything!

From this general place of feeling good comes step three. Pretend that your life is the way you want it to be. Write it down, draw a picture. Make a vision board. Ignore the current situation that is making you feel down. Don't talk about it, don't sit down and try to figure out why it happened and what you can do to not let it happen again. Talk about the way you want to feel and be as if it is the truth now and has already manifested. Even if you sound crazy. It doesn't matter! This is how it works. For example, if you're sick say things like, "I'm healthy as can be. I'm in the peak of my health. I feel alive, I feel vital, I feel easy, I feel free, I feel bright, I feel full of life. I feel simple, I feel comfortable. I feel magical. I'm at the top of my game. I feel one with my inner being and Source energy!" Say something like this out loud to yourself. Do it for as little as 17 seconds, and then watch how other words that match what you are talking about easily come and start to make you feel good. It's from that place of generally feeling good that more good things on every subject will come to you. You have get out of the way of the problem and focus purely on the feeling of what you want. Use any subject in the world. Do you get it? It may be difficult at first, but if you do this process long enough you will start to see your mood and perspective on the world around you shift quickly. You will feel the shift at first through your emotions, then the physical manifestation of what you want is right around the corner. If you are feeling bad, try saying more general things such as: "Things are always working out for me. I'm strong and powerful and I know my life is always changing. Other people have been where I am now and are now thriving. I got this. I can do this. I will do this. I am healthy. I am alive. I am powerful." By talking to yourself in this general way, you will start to feel good because you're not focusing on anything specific that makes you feel bad. From this place of feeling good, do whatever you need to do with the attitude that things are always working out for you. Even though you may be in a place you don't want to be, you are on your way. And you get there by doing anything, anything in the world that makes you feel good in that moment. Remember, it's the emotions and feelings you are reaching for that you need to focus on. Your emotions are your guides to let you know whether you are on your path, or have deviated from it. Have no fear, for you can get right back on your path by focusing on anything that assists you in feeling good. Do not focus on the "big problems" unless you are specifically doing your deep dark work with your healer. Set a time during the week or day when you can focus directly on the core issue with the intention of realizing it fully, healing it, and letting it go. This refers back to Chapter Four, and the process of doing your deep dark work. Maybe you have no idea why you are feeling negative emotion. Sometimes, it is just a thought pattern. Sometimes it's because of past trauma. Mostly, it's your undone deep dark work.

To change something that is unwanted, you have to do the work. Just reading this book isn't enough. You can't just think about this and understand it intellectually. You have to feel it and do your part. If there is deep dark work that is ready to be dealt with, your body might make you sick in order to get your attention. What is being triggered by the illness is saying: "Hey! Pay attention to me! I'm ready to be healed and released, please!" A personal example is that I once had a very vivid and intense dream that made me feel horrible emotionally. A few days after the dream I became very ill. I am blessed to know a beautiful energy healer, Deloris. (I love you and thank you, Deloris.) My intuition was telling me the dream was the reason for my illness, so she and I focused our work there. It ended up being a dream about a past life where I did horrible things to other people. After I did my work and released this past life and dream, I felt better almost instantly. It doesn't matter if the dream or past life was real or made up. Because after I did my work and healed myself I felt like a brand new person, with more clarity and health than before I got sick. No medicine, no doctors. I did nothing other than going all the way with my deep dark work. This is my process: find the key, step through the door, shine the light, heal and realize whatever it is inside the door, close the door, and vanish the key and the door into pure light love Source energy. It might not be the same for you, or maybe it could be. It all depends on you. Listen to your body, it will always tell you what you need to heal and grow.

No matter how horrible you think your life is now, I tell you from the bottom of my heart things will get better for you. You've got this. The power that creates worlds lives within you. You are loved, you are valued, and you are God; you are pure Source energy in a body. Focus purely on how you want to be and feel. Pretend or see what you want in your mind, and bask in the deliciousness of how its feels to have the things and feelings you want. You can get through this, I believe in you, and so does the Source within you. Ask for help, and you shall receive it. Stop trying so damn hard. Give yourself a break!

So many people are sick. So many people are well. What do you want to focus on? Sickness or wellness? Love or fear? We currently live in a society run by a government that uses fear to control. It creates food, substances, and pills to intentionally make you sick. The news is all about mind control. If those in charge can make you feel afraid and powerless, they can control you. I stopped watching the news many years ago. It's all bullshit. The world isn't going to disappear. There will never be a disease that kills off everyone. There will always be enough food and water. If you say, "I'm going to live my life in perfect health and healing until the day I leave this body," and believe it in every cell of your body, then it must be so. If you eat something and think it's bad for you, it will be bad for you. If you know something is bad for you and do it anyway, it will be bad for you. Do anything and say it is good for you, it will be good. You have the power. You are the creator of your own reality. I can't say this enough. If "what is" is not what you want, ignore it. Ignore whatever you currently do not want, and focus on the wellness, wholeness, vitality and life in your body. This is how you become well. It's a "mind-vibration-feeling" game. It's possible to make a sickness go away by not giving it a single moment of attention. It is possible to live a life of perfect health until the day you die. You don't have to grow old, get sick, and suffer until you die. It is possible to die mindfully and without pain, sitting upright in a meditation pose if you wanted to. Just because others suffer and are in pain doesn't mean you have to also. Personalize your life, personalize your death. You are the author of your life story. Nobody else. Sickness and depression can be tools on our path to doing our deep dark work and finding deeper enlightenment with who we really are and why we have come. You hear stories all the time of people almost dying, but then they recover and live out an amazing, joyful life. Sometimes you need to go way down to go way up. You don't have to, but some people need this journey. The journey is personal, and many paths lead to the same place.

: PROTECTING YOURSELF :

In Chicago where I'm from, there are over 2 million people as of 2016. That's a lot of people. All kinds of thoughts and energy are going around all over the place. Have you ever found yourself having a wonderful day, in a good mood, you have that extra skip in your step, and then all of a sudden you start to think negative thoughts, or start to feel negative emotion in your body? Often when this happens you are feeling other people's thoughts and energy, not yours. It's

70

your neighbors across the street. It's the people fighting who live above you. It's a person that walked past you on the street. You are picking up on the thoughts and energy of others. As we live and interact with people in this world, we need to have a sense of protection.

Let me be very clear here: with this protection you are not focusing specifically on what it is you are trying to keep away from you. Instead, you protect your energy in a general way from all the other stuff that people might be dealing with and unconsciously putting out into the world. People leak out energy and spread it around like a wildfire. This is nothing to be concerned about. Other people have no power over your thoughts or well-being unless you allow it. You are in charge. If you want to connect to another person, animal, or plant, it's up to you to let their energy connect with yours. So all the things you might label "bad energy," "bad people," or "psychic vampires" have no power over you, ever. They have no influence whatsoever unless you focus on them and invite their energy in. You could do this consciously or unconsciously.

There is no need to tell anyone about this protection you have. You don't need to talk to anyone about anything related to your spiritual path or practice if you don't want to. You don't have to explain or justify anything to anyone for that matter. Feel the relief of this statement from Source. Aaaaahhhh, exhale. So nice, isn't it? There is no need to have anybody understand your life or why you're doing what you're doing. Let go of the attachment to the outcome of what you want. Just enjoy this moment as it is. Trust that you are moving towards that which you want. Let life unfold naturally the way it does for all living beings on this earth. Your life will unfold as soon as you get out of your own way, do your deep dark work, and commit to spiritual practice.

Getting back to the matter of generally protecting yourself from the thoughts and energy of others, I'll explain what I do to protect myself. It's not even really "protecting," but more like staying with my energy only and not allowing myself to be influenced by other people's energies, thoughts, or projections. So be very general and easy with all this. Here we go! As you begin your day, before you leave your house or talk to anybody, close your eyes and imagine you are sitting in the center of a white circular crystal light surrounding your body. There is nothing but Divine light love positive energy in and around you, and coming from you while you are in this circle of light. Imagine it, see it, feel it. You can even create the circle of white light with your breath and hands. You can call upon specific helpers and guides to be with you throughout your day as well. This can take a few seconds, or minutes. You can do it sitting down, laying down, or standing up. Make it personal. When you're done say "thank you" and, boom! You are protected from all stuff you don't want. You don't need to think about all the negative stuff out there that you don't want to affect you or be taken from you. Just protect yourself, and your guides and your body will do the rest.

Remember, if you're feeling any negative emotion, or dealing with something unwanted, go general with your thoughts and emotions. Be simple with your thoughts and words. Focus on general words that make you feel good. Words like "easy," "simple," "calm," "comfortable," "loved," and so on.

When you're feeling good inside be as specific as possible, while still maintaining that sense of feeling happy and good. With this type of protection always go general while creating it, because when you're thinking about things you don't want to be thinking about, you're already thinking about them! So don't even bring it up! This will help you to stay grounded in your body, with your energy only. You choose whose energy you want to connect with and who you let in your circle, your lover, pet, nature, best friend, business partner, teacher, healer, for instance. You have control over everything in your life. You are a creator. You get to create and experience whatever you want. Nobody has power over you. Do you understand that? Nobody! Unless you believe they do, then they do. Get it? Good!

: 7 :

THE "WHAT ABOUT ME?!" TRIP

Everyone is obsessed with themselves, and rightfully so. You are Source energy in a body. You are the energy that is Jesus the Christ and the Buddha. You are the pure positive light love energy that creates worlds. The elements are in your body. The universe is in your body. You have been given this human body to live out your soul's intention, to feel pleasure and fun now. We are all creators, here to make art with everything we say and do. You have been given your senses to deeply create and experience pleasure in ways no other being in the entire universe can. So you should be obsessed with your life, to a certain extent. Many people get lost with their power. Most of them are obsessed with their thoughts, bodies, ego, what other people think about them, what happened in the past, and what might happen in the future. People love to talk about themselves all the time. "What's your opinion on this subject? Let's talk about what happened to you yesterday, a year ago, when you were a kid, this conversation with that person, what's going on with your kids, and what's your opinion about this and that. Why do you think this happened? I'm so worried about this! Did you hear about so and so doing this and that?" It is endless. People love to plan for the future. Plan the vacation, plan the wedding, the big birthday party, the next meal. People love to talk. Everyone loves the sound of their own voice. People love drama and talking about other people's lives, and offering opinions about everything. They talk about themselves and gossip all day long. Gossip, gossip, gossip. It is very important to understand that your thoughts are just a sequence of recycled past information, endless gossip, and imagination.

"Me me me me me me me, what about me?!" This is everyone's favorite song to sing. Social media and entertainment industries have capitalized on a world revolved around making an individual's ego the most important thing on the planet. Television shows, movies, magazines, music, games, and beauty and health products are all about focusing on you and other people's lives in an extremely egotistical way. Social media is the master of this. You have your personal Facebook page, your Instagram, your Tweets, your blog, your Snapchat, your opinion on this topic and that person. It never ends. People are obsessed with taking selfies. Let's take a picture while I eat ice cream, while I walk down the street, hanging out with my friends, while I take a shit, while I do this yoga pose on a rock on the beach. You get it. It's all about you. Making the ego the master, the star of the show called "life." At the top of your news feed, Facebook asks "What's on your mind?" Facebook is all about being the "Social Network," when in reality its news feed is the most anti-social thing ever created. You can spend hours scrolling through your news feed, 95 percent of which is pointless trivialities you neither care about nor really need to know. You're on the couch or in bed and you log onto Facebook because you're bored. Boom! An hour passed. I have been guilty of this, we all have. You don't need to know what other people think or feel and or interested in all the time, do you? Do you really care? Of course you care what your closest friends think, your lover, and your family, yes. But that's really it. You should only really have like 10 to 30 friends on Facebook or Instagram, right? But we have hundreds or thousands. It seems like some sort of power trip to have followers on social media networks. It gives people a false sense of worthiness and popularity. Whoever has the most likes or followers is winning at life, right? People believe this false reality.

Nowadays, popular music and movies are all about worshipping the individual and the ego. Song themes are: "Why did you do this to me? I feel this. I don't like this, I do like that. I want this, I don't want that. I think this, I think that. Why did you break my heart? I want to grind you up in the club. Me me me me me." The Bravo television network is literally a channel all about drama. Reality television, an ironic name considering it is the furthest perspective from true reality, is all about making viewers invest their time, energy, and money on other people who are living their life on a screen. There is so much focus on other people's drama, stress, relationships, and sex life. People believe that drama, gossip, sex, buying things, stress, fighting, making money, and arguing is normal life just because that's what movies, television, magazines, and music are showing you. And then you say, "Well this must be real life because it's a reality TV show! This must be how to live life because that's how it's done in the movies. Brad Pitt is doing it, wearing it, saying it, buying it, so I want it too! People on TV are always stressed out, so it must be normal for me to always be stressed out. That song by the pop singer who sells out stadiums is singing about this and that so it must be true. They said this and that on the news, so it must be true. This larger-than-life famous person is doing this and saying this and wearing this. I want to be like them, and look like them, and live that life! Look how happy they are! They have so much money and women and all the stuff!" All lies! This is all misplaced identification.

You have become programmed to think and live a certain way. This way is based completely on the ego and materialism, a view and lifestyle where the whole world revolves around you in a negative way. Ego and mind become God. You separate yourself from everything that is not related to your body, thoughts, emotions and ego. "This is me, that is not me. I am this person, with this identity, who wants these things, and only I matter, nothing else does." You want this thing and that relationship, to live this lifestyle and look that way, and have this type of sexy body because that is what the media tells you. And when you don't feel happy living this way you feel unworthy, ugly, and poor. People try to center their happiness around material objects, other people, and specific conditions. That is totally backwards from the truth. Relationships or objects alone cannot make anyone happy. People chase things, relationships, status, and when they get them they have attained nothing but whatever the thing is. They wind up sad or broke, and need a pill to make them happy and then become a slave. Then one day they wake up to the truth, or they die. And the people in charge don't want us to awaken and find enlightenment. They want us to be zombies, to not think for ourselves and continue working for the man. Lifetime after lifetime after lifetime.

This is happening to people all over the world. And it all driven by a massive corporate money-making machine. You might say it's all just entertainment, right? Everyone is entitled to live their own individual unique life, right? That does not appear to be true when so many people chase money, sex, and fame, but yet feel so fearful and hopeless on the inside. You are made to think this is how you are supposed to live, act, look, and feel; that this is the path to happiness. When really these are all unrealistic beliefs and unattainable goals. It's all false hope. Living this way only makes people feel unhappy and hopeless, like they are broken and ruined. The CEO of a major company with the trophy wife, sports cars in the garage, millions of dollars, lots of friends, and all the stuff might be the most unhappy person in the entire world. Remember, everything is about balance, intention, and perspective.

I'm not saying that having things and looking good and enjoying entertainment is altogether a bad thing. I like to look and dress a certain way. I like having money. I like nice things. I enjoy driving fast cars. I love to travel and spend money on nice things that I desire. I like the cheesy romantic comedies from the 90's and early 2000's. However, for me these are purely for entertainment and pleasure. They are simply used as tools to feel good. I know these things are just here for me to feel better than I already do now. I am not allowing them to shape my thoughts or my lifestyle in an unhealthy way. How wonderful it is to have all these different things to use and enjoy! What a gift! I have been on both ends of the stick with this lifestyle, and I now know the difference. I have been hypnotized by the money making trendy sex driven lifestyle. As a teen, all I used to care about was getting high, becoming a rock star, and getting laid. In my early twenties it was all about making money. What I'm saying is that it is okay to desire and own things. That is part of the reason why you incarnate into this physical experience, to enjoy the sensory experience of the physical manifestation of whatever you want. But it's not just about the having it in physical form. You must get happy first. Then enjoy things and people, instead of expecting things and people to make you happy and whole. That's what it all comes down to. Life is supposed to be fun and pleasurable. We have come for the whole process of creation. Most people create unconsciously, unaware that thoughts actually manifest into physical reality. It is so much more enjoyable when you are in on the process every step of the way! You came here to deliberately create what you want, not to have other people or governments decide who you are and what you want! In America, people worship things and other people and God comes somewhere towards the end of the list. In the east, like India, God comes first. People can have nothing, but still be extremely spiritual, loving, and happy as can be. Interesting, isn't it? So, how do you want to live your life? Again, you have to make all this personal, because you are in control of everything. Everything! Even all those unwanted conditions in your life are there to help you clarify what you do want. Make peace with the contrast for it is your best friend.

Now, let me clarify further. Entertainment and social media are not always negative. Music is a massive part of my existence. Facebook is a wonderful way to stay connected with loved ones. I love seeing other people's Instagram pictures of nature and things I am also interested in. It all just comes down to balance and perspective. Many people base their worthiness on social media and outside objects. This is the "high school mindset." It's that mindset of "who is friends with whom, who has what new item first, who's wearing what, who is dating whom, did you hear about this and that? What are you doing this weekend? Why aren't you doing this? You going to that big party on Friday? Blah, Blah, Blah." Is this really living? It's a distraction from seeing your deep dark work and really getting down with God. It can be intense and scary when you begin to sit still and be silent with your thoughts; to see your deep dark work clearly and hear the inner child cry for help. Nobody really wants to do this at first. The high school mindset is an excuse for being too busy for your spiritual practice. It's the lazy way to live. Smart phones and social media are a major distraction to the spiritual path. They can completely pull people out of the present moment. Notification after notification. Check this, now do that, now text them back, now check your email, then call this person, look at this thing, take a picture, write another text, play this game, look at this blog or article, write a Facebook comment, post another video, watch another kitten video, post another selfie. It all sucks up a lot of time! One can lose sight very quickly of what really matters. Life turns into this power trip of "what about me."

Now I am here to say: What about nature? What about God? What about having a face-to-face and heartfelt conversation with someone? What about the present moment? What about this magical life happening all around you? What about sitting still and feeling the aliveness of your inner body and pleasure of your breath?

You see, there has to be a balance. Try meditating for 15 minutes, and then answer some texts and check emails. Walk your dog without your phone. Then maybe look at Instagram for a bit. Go and interact with someone in person. Look into each other's eyes, not your phones. Watch a movie, then chant for 20 minutes. Clean the house mindfully, as if you were cleaning it for God herself. Everything you do, no matter how mundane it is, can be turned into a spiritual practice if you're doing it mindfully and with love in your heart. There has to be balance. Take the mundane everyday existence of life and make it sacred and holy. Everything is sacred and holy. Everyone is God. So I turn off the push notifications on my smart phone. I'm not saying they are bad, but for some people all those notifications are really just taking you out of the present moment, and turning your attention to the ego. The notifications, texts, and emails are saying, "Stop what you are doing! Pay attention to this!" If your phone is a tool for your work or spiritual practice then you can look at your apps, texts and emails in a mindful way. Next time you get a text message, pause before reading it. Take a few deep breaths. Center yourself. Get into your Now, and from that place read the text. Do whatever you want with your smartphone or social media. Just do it mindfully, with awareness and balanced action. And be aware what effect it has on you and how it makes you feel inside. Know why you are doing something and do it mindfully. Be aware if it is adding to your life in a positive way, or taking away. That's all I'm saying.

I think technology is a beautiful thing. I love it. Youtube, GPS, and iTunes are things I use everyday. But I use them mindfully and in balance with my spiritual practices. I even use technology to assist my spiritual practices. I have an awesome meditation app on my phone that I use all the time. Social media is a great way to promote your service and connect with other like-minded people. Many wonderful teachers out there are sharing their wisdom on social media and the internet. YouTube channels, blogs, websites, you name it. So awesome! What a gift to have such quick and easy access to all this information!

Now is the greatest time to be alive! There is a great awakening in our world presently. More enlightened and mindful human beings exist now than ever before. We are waking up to a new paradigm. It's wonderful and exciting! But a massive number of people are still living in unbalanced and unhealthy ways, perhaps because they are unaware of their options or just don't know another way to live. I believe it is because people do not know how to handle their bodies, thoughts, emotions, and energies. Many of them don't have a clue on what to do with this powerful mechanism called the human body. This body did not come with a handbook on how to live this birth for all it's worth, which is why I created one. The teachings in this book should be taught to every child in every school all over the world. The Buddha said one of the greatest paths to suffering is ignorance. Some people just don't know that there is more to life than how many likes their selfie gets on Facebook. There is more to life than making money, going to school, getting a job having a nice looking body, finding the perfect mate, having kids, working hard, getting sick, and dying. They don't know there are other options, other ways of thinking and being a human on Earth, and different ways to connect with people. If you are one of these people, you now know there is another way.

What you want to do next is your choice, and yours alone. There is no right or wrong here, no good or bad. However there is truth, and there are lies. Surround yourself with the truth as much as possible in all aspects of your life. By truth, I mean whatever creates positive good feelings within you when you focus on them. From the music you listen to to the people you hang out with and conversate with. What you see, what you hear, what you say, all has to be in union with the truth. With God. With love.

If what I have said so far resonates with you, and you want more to life than what you thought was possible, then you have to create that balance and life you want. Create your spiritual practice. Find the God within you. Find the name of God that works for you. Create your God. What is her/his/its name? Find it. You are it. Fall in love with love and yourself in a mindful healthy way. Be devoted to being your true self. Like whatever it is you like, whatever it is you are into, whatever sports team or movie star you follow, but do it without identifying who you are with it. Do it all without losing yourself in the game. Be yourself and follow your bliss. Maybe you just want to be a good person. Then that's enough. Maybe it's making an app. Or designing a video game. Or working for Hollywood or MTV or Bravo. Whatever your dream or passion is, go for it! Make it your primary intention everyday. Follow your path, not someone else's. Do what you truly want to do, from your heart. Find the balance of using the wonderful gifts and tools that other humans have made to help serve yourself, and serve others. If you want to look like Brad Pitt, do it, but do it because every cell in your body knows that this is what you want to do to express your true self. Do everything mindfully. Know why you are doing what you are doing. See everything clearly. You are in control of what you like, do, and desire to be, not corporations and media. Let everyone else in your life be themselves as well. Try not to control other people. The same goes for your children. You are in control on how much influence the media and the entertainment industry has on your children's evolution and development. If you have three young kids for instance, and they love playing video games, let them! But set boundaries and limits. Also get them involved with other things they like, such as sports or gymnastics. Go on camping trips with them. Teach them about nature, love, and energy. Let them play their video games on your iPad, but maybe not at dinner with the family. Maybe use it as a reward for doing well in school. You get my point.

Life is about balance, with your loved ones and your spiritual practice. Too much of anything creates imbalance, and with imbalance comes suffering. When you are in the moment, aligned with the Source energy that creates worlds, you will know when you are in or out of balance and what to do about it. Just ask. Is what you are paying attention to beneficial to your healing and growth? Or is it hindering you to some degree? Listen to your body and your emotions, these you can trust. If what you are paying attention to is making you feel bad, then that is a sign to stop. Change the channel, stop watching the movie, listen to something else, ignore what is going on around you or remove yourself from the situation. Or try thinking about it in a different way. If what you are giving your attention to feels good, do more of that. I repeat topics and points that are very important so you can see how this is all connected. You do. If you need a teacher to help you practice all this then seek a teacher who has mastered these teachings. Find one who can take your hand and guide you to whatever you want to attain, or help you get rid of.

So you go from a place of only caring about you, your needs and desires, to caring about you and your relationship with Source, family, friends, nature, energy, community, and so on. Go from checking your Facebook page for a bit to your meditation practice. However it is possible to reverse all this and your spiritual and meditation practice could be your main imbalance. If you just meditate all the time, only do your yoga practice and spiritual work, and don't connect with people and the outside world, then there is still an imbalance. Be in the world, but not attached to it. Do whatever it is you are doing, but do it with awareness and presence in the moment. Stay connected to yourself by staying connected to your breath, thoughts, and actions. Do whatever you want! Just know clearly what you are doing, and be mindful with everything you say, think, and do. This all happens through practice. Our entire life is a practice. You are doing well. So are your kids and younger generation. Keep the social media and the internet. You don't have to delete your Facebook page and get rid of your smartphone. Just pay attention to what you are giving your attention to and how it makes you feel inside. Or maybe you do need to get rid of your smartphone to find your balance. If you are present in the moment and doing something that feels good, do it. If you don't feel good, don't do it. There is nothing that you are supposed to be doing. You can't get this wrong. There's no right way to live. There is what you declare to be "right" based on how it makes you feel. Focus on you. Let other people be them. Listen to your body and remember this: You are not truly anything that is outside of you. You are connected to everything, but you are not these things entirely. You are not your body. You are not your mind. You are not the things you have gathered in your life. You are made of energy. Energy and vibration that can not be described with words. The human mind can not wrap itself around topics related to non-physical Source energy. For words don't truly teach. Only by living your life in association with the truth and flowing with the laws of the universe will you then become the master. We are all in this together, as one.

: PART III :

Ok, did you survive all that? Yes, you did! See, it wasn't so bad right? Now it's time to create and fine tune your spiritual and meditation practice. I will talk about what it means to be spiritual and feel enlightened, and from there we will invoke the master! We will focus on creating healthy balanced relationships with yourself, other people, and with nature. Lastly, we will discuss the illusion of fear and how to awaken to the power of who you are and what you're all about! Smile and laugh out loud! This is going to be fun, you will love it! I promise!

: 8 :

CUSTOMIZING YOUR
SPIRITUAL & MEDITATION
PRACTICE

So you are presently working on or have done your deep dark work. It's now time to deepen your meditation and spiritual practice. You can start meditating and living a spiritual life at any point on your life journey and at any age. There is no right or wrong time to begin a spiritual practice and establish your own unique relationship to God. Meditation is a powerful tool to realize your deep dark work, learn how your mind works, become present in the Now, gain insight and wisdom, connect with your guides, relax, find stillness without and within, and find peace and connection to the Divine nature within your heart. When you become quiet inside, you begin to hear your truth. Trust what you hear and use it to gain clarity to do the work that needs to be done. Through meditation I became aware of my deep dark work at a young age, but I was too scared to work on it then. Over time the negative emotions and energy grew inside me and dominated my mind and body until the deep dark work made me feel horrible, physically and mentally. It was trying to get my attention to heal it, learn from it, and let it go. And it worked! Since I have faced my deep dark work, my life has shifted in such powerful positive ways that I can not even describe in words. So there is no right time to work on yourself. You are always working on yourself. If you don't feel the time is right this moment, so be it. Only you can decide when to start doing your true work and living the life you were born to live. But if you are consciously aware of the darkness right now, and it's not going away as you read this, then you might as well start now!

A spiritual practice has to be customized and personal to fit you. As you can see, that is the theme for all this. You have got to make your life journey personal. Many people take on other people's ways and spiritual practices. Yes, while you can choose and connect with something that has been done before, like yoga asana or Buddhism for example, you still have to personalize it and make it work for you. Do not take somebody else's spiritual journey and follow it step-by-step or word-for-word. You have to make it accessible and appropriate for you based on where you live and what you are doing with your life. If you are a business and family man working in New York City, then sitting in a cave and meditating all day is probably not going to be an easy task, nor make sense to you. That doesn't mean you can never do it if you feel that path calling you, but currently where you are now, it may not work. You get this, yes? Wherever you currently are is where you start. Because you have to start somewhere, and it has to be now. If where you currently live does not suit where you truly want to be, in order to live the life you want and pursue the spiritual practices you want to experience, then travel or move to a place that will fulfill your desires. Maybe take a pilgrimage to India like so many people do. You don't have to move somewhere, you can visit and see what's right for you. If you feel you have to relocate, do this as soon as possible. Find the place of feeling good, listen to the impulse and follow it. If you are doing anything from a place of not feeling good, don't act. If you feel anxious, scared, fearful, or angry, then it is not the time to act upon a decision. Find that place of calm and ease, and from that place listen to your impulses, to your heart and gut.

There are many spiritual practices that have been created on this planet. If you feel the calling to follow one already laid out, then do so with all of your heart and soul. There may come a day when you might not connect with that practice anymore. And so you create or find another path that is suitable to who you are, where you are, and what you want. I have studied and practiced many different forms of religions and spiritual practices. None of them stuck completely. I choose what I want to connect with from these practices and make them my own. I personalize them to what I want and to what I believe to be true within myself. I can't take anyone else's word on anything. I have to experience it to be true for myself and through living life. I wish the same for you.

One of the most important spiritual practices is meditation, which is accessible to all humans. All the different spiritual practices and rituals are based on the practice of meditation, which is really practicing mindfulness. It is training yourself to be present and enjoy life moment to moment. In this chapter I will discuss what I consider meditation and mindfulness to be, and various ways to start a meditation practice or evolve an existing one.

: WHAT IS MEDITATION & WHY DO IT :

Meditation is finding the place in your mind and body that is fully present and aware in the Now. It is seeing things clearly, as they are, in the moment, without any physical or mental resistance or attachment to your experience. It involves bringing yourself to a place of pure momentary awareness without needing to change that moment or hold onto it. You watch thoughts and images enter your mind and leave, or hear the sounds come and go. It is present, moment to moment awareness. It's like looking up at the sky, and watching a bird fly by. You see it with your eyes and hear it with your ears. You might feel it if it poops on you. You might feel appreciation for the beauty of the animal. But then the bird flies away, and that's that. You're not going to sit there and cry and wish the bird stayed longer, and think about that bird for the rest of your day, and try to figure out what was the real meaning behind seeing this bird. Where did it go? Why did that happen to me? What's going on here?

I'm exaggerating a bit, but the same goes for watching the thoughts and sensations arise and fall in your body during meditation and waking life. It's that simple. This is why it is important to heal your deep dark work from this life or past lives. When you sit in stillness, and see your thoughts and feel your body clearly, you will begin to see and feel all that deep dark stuff that has been hiding away. You will see and feel all the negative emotions that need to be worked on and healed. They won't go away until you do! This is very important, my friends. You can ignore them all you want. But if they keep showing up, there's a reason for it. The deep dark work might show up in the form of thoughts, feelings, or physical bodily aches and pains. The sensations may be heightened when you are meditating because you are calming your mind and slowing your thought processes. When you are thinking and focusing on your thoughts and actions your deep dark work gets covered up momentary. You get distracted by your thoughts and actions and hide away from your deep dark work. Meditation shows you the truth of every subject at every level. So it is important to listen to your mind and body when it shows you these things, and do the work so you can start meditating with comfort and joy. You will discover who you really are and begin to live out your life's purpose!

As you begin addressing your deep dark work, or once it is done, you can feel the space within where the universe dwells. The space between the thoughts is a place of peace and pure awareness. It is the positive love Source energy that creates worlds. You feel it in the aliveness of your inner body, the pleasure of the breath and your senses. Meditation is needed to help us become present in the Now, where all those positive emotions and feelings dwell. The most basic meditation practice is to just sit and watch your breath for any length of time. This is necessary to finding your center, the place of calm, love, and ease that is within us all. If you look at pictures or statues of the masters, such as the Buddha or Shiva, they are usually sitting in a meditation posture. Meditation is how we train our minds to let go of controlling our lives, and to see our truth. You just sit and focus only on you, not anything else going on in your life. Just you. Everything you are shows up in meditation. The good, the bad, and the ugly.

By now you know that you are not your thoughts. You are neither the thinking mind nor just a body. We use thinking and thought to live life as humans and to function. We connect with each other to co-create, to feel alive and pleasure through our bodies. But thought and thinking is not life. Many people experience "monkey-mind." We need to tame the monkey, people! The monkey-mind takes over everything. The movie Planet Of The Apes is real and happening right now in people's heads. They chase thoughts here and there, everywhere. We fight wars and chase desire after desire! Can you find a place where you are not completely absorbed by every thought and idea you have? Have not identified who you are with it? Through meditation we learn to use the mind to find the feelings that we are all yearning for, feelings like love, joy, power, pleasure, joy and fun. I am specifically referring to sitting meditation. It all begins there. The process of sitting and mastering how your mind works could take one day, or it may take years. The good news is that you have your entire life to work on it. It all depends on you, what you are ready for, and how much time you spend practicing. All this being said, you can see the importance of practicing meditation. I will now share with you practices that have worked for me.

: FIRST THINGS FIRST: SETTING YOUR MEDITATION SPACE :

Before you begin to meditate, you will need somewhere to sit. Find a place in your home that you declare to be a temple. It can be a corner in your living room or bedroom, or an entire room. Once you find that space, then it's time to create a sacred altar. On your altar and the wall above, place pictures of people who you admire or respect. They can be pictures of people you love or pictures of people you consider masters of something you want to master yourself. They can be teachers, gurus, saints and sages, angels, or masters of anything. On my altar I have stones and crystals, mala beads, and gifts acquired over time that I consider sacred. I have pictures of my family, statues, and pictures of Shiva, Buddha, B.K.S. Iyengar, Jesus, Anandamayi Ma, and Kali to name a few. You can put anything you want on this altar, anything you consider sacred. Placing a lit candle on your altar before you meditate is a nice way to represent the power of the Divine and bring the sacred energy alive. Personalize it! There is no right or wrong way to make an altar. The most important thing is that this altar space is the most sacred thing to you besides your body and loved ones. It is so because you declare it to be. You can have a random rock on your altar, and if you consider it sacred, it is. You can have a grain of rice on your altar, and if you see God in that rice, it's sacred. It's all about intention and what you see, not what others see. You make things sacred. You are creator! You are inviting God to meet you at this altar every time you sit down, light your candle, and bow. This is a place you can retreat to for refuge. This is your own sacred temple. Your body is sacred temple number one; your space and altar are number two. This is a place you can cry, laugh, scream, meditate, pray, ask for guidance and help, sing, chant, bow, and give gratitude and appreciation. And because you have declared this space and altar sacred and holy, when your human bone temple meets this sacred space temple, very magical and powerful things manifest. It is a meeting of Gods, creator meeting creation.

: GENERAL TECHNIQUES FOR ALL MEDITATION :

It is important to note here, that I believe the purpose for meditation is to become nothing. To become the void of nothingness. To be fully present in your body without the need and desire to do anything. Meditation is not a time for creation. Not a time to figure things out. Nor a time to make anything happen. You may receive insight, wisdom, or feel energy flowing through your body during or after you meditation, but don't sit for that specific purpose. You are sitting to just be, to become present and receptive. For it is from that place of receptivity that you receive the good thoughts and ideas, the good feeling emotions, and the impulses to create and act. Of course, you can set any intention you want before you meditate, such as finding clarity to a question. But what I am saying is to make your meditation about allowing yourself to soften into a nothingness state of being in the present moment, which will automatically put you in a vibration of allowing and receiving. In that state of ease and receptivity, what you seek will find you. The three basic meditation practices described below are ways to assist you in reaching this natural vibration.

That said, begin your meditation with setting an intention. Why are you going to sit, and for how long? Decide on the length of time you will be meditating. Nowadays there are smartphone apps you can use to time your meditations. Start easy. Try three minutes. When that becomes somewhat easy, add time. Try five minutes, then 10 minutes, 15, 20, 30 and so on. Fifteen minutes is a good time for a regular practice time. You can add and subtract time, but I feel 15 minutes is the perfect amount of time to move into the energy you are reaching for though the meditation.

Once your timer is set, focus on the emotions you want to feel during and after your mediation. Once you're in that place of feeling good, then you should to ground yourself. You can ask your guides for help staying grounded and aligned in your body, or visualize yourself being grounded in whatever way you choose. The practice I use to ground is to pretend I am a tree. I lie down or sit up straight, and imagine roots are growing out of my pelvis and digging deep down into the Earth's core. I visualize this as I exhale. Through my breath I feel my roots wrap around the core of Mother Earth. I continue to visualize my roots wrapped around the core as I inhale and bring my awareness back into my body. When your intention is set, your timer is ready, you feel the emotions you want to feel, and you are grounded, then you are almost ready to begin meditating.

Be sure you are sitting upright and that you are comfortable. Comfort is key. Put on extra clothing if you are cold. You may need to sit on a bolster, yoga block, blanket, or pillow so you are able to sit up straight with the natural curvature of your spine. If you need to sit on a chair or stool, that's fine as well. You are still a spiritual person even if you can't sit in a cross-legged position. In time, you can even meditate lying down. Customize your experience. When you sit you want to feel your ears directly above the plain of your shoulders, in line with your hips. Position your legs in any way that works for you. Apply this to any type of seated meditation. Are you comfy? Good!

Next comes the breath. This breathing technique applies to all three of the meditation practices below. Feel your breath and breathe naturally and slowly. Let your breath do whatever it wants, and focus on your exhalations more than your inhalations. Your inhalations will take care of themselves. Focus on gentle, soft, full exhalations. Allow your body to relax as you exhale, but maintain just enough effort to continue sitting up straight with ease. Make sure your head and shoulders don't fall forward.

: 3 BASIC POWERFUL MEDITATION PRACTICES FOR EVERYONE :

I will lay out three basic seated meditations that have worked for me, and I believe can work for anyone. When I say they worked for me, I mean that this practice enabled me to clearly see the deep dark work that needed to be done. I learned how my mind and body work. These practices assisted me in becoming present in the moment, and in feeling the aliveness of my inner body which is always filled with bliss and love. The three meditation practices can be used as tools to help create your own sitting practice. Be kind and compassionate with yourself through all this. At first you might just sit there and be thinking about stuff the entire time. That's fine. The fact that you are aware that you are thinking is a big step. The "you" that is watching and realizing your thoughts is the "you" to focus on. It will get easier the more you practice and the clearer your intention becomes. Remember, it is impossible to stop thought completely. That's not what you are trying to do here. You want to find the space between the thoughts. Find the stillness and emptiness between the thoughts. Feel and see that space, and over time the space expands for as long as you want it to. Be playful and humble with it all. This is not a job, nor something you have to do. You are doing this because you want to master yourself and feel good, that's all. Are you ready? Yeah you are! So let's go!

: CANDLE STARING :

In this practice you will light a candle and stare at the flame. Sounds simple, right? Begin by following the general guidelines I outlined in the previous section: find your space, set up your altar, sit comfortably, set your intention and get grounded. Be sure to follow the breathing technique I explained.

Feel your breath and stare at the flame. You want the flame to be on your altar if possible, and at a level so that you are not looking up but your gaze is slightly downward. The candle should be placed a distance away from you that is comfortable to look at, around 24 to 36 inches. Stare at the flame of the candle, and feel your natural breath moving through your nose. Tell your mind, "Okay mind, I know you can focus, now focus on this candle." You can apply that to any meditation where you want to focus on a single point like a candle, breath, or a repetitive sound. Let your eyes relax and soften, they are neither completely open nor closed. See the candle for what it is: the light of Source, the light and power of creation and destruction. Thoughts and sensations will come. Notice them, and bring your attention back to looking at the flame, through the flame. There is nothing to figure out and nothing to do other than looking at the flame. Your mind and eyes will wander, bring your attention back to the flame. Remember, you are training yourself to be present in the moment, not trying to go anywhere or reach some divine God-state. We already are that divine God energy, and you are exactly where you are supposed to be. You are going inward to see it and know it fully. It never goes away, and never dims. Source energy is you, you are the candle, you are love. You are God. See the candle, stare at it, ignore your thoughts. You can even label your thoughts as "thoughts" or "thinking" as they arise. That's all.

After a few minutes of staring at the flame, close your eyes and see the flame in your mind's eye. Feel the fire within

99

your own heart. It is the fire of Source that is waiting there wanting you to feel it, experience it, and be it! Your mind will wander; kindly bring it back. Do this practice to help your mind soften, and train it to focus on one thing in the moment rather than a thousand things from the past or the future. Play with staring at the flame, closing your eyes and seeing the flame in your mind, then opening your eyes again. Repeat this as often as you like. Try not to quit your mediation early. I promise the timer will go off, and you can do this! Once your timer goes off, pause for a few moments. Reflect on your experience without judgment, or try journaling. Decide whether the time was too long or short, and take note for next time. Good job! Repeat this practice every morning for at least 7-30 days.

: EXPERIENCE THE GIFT OF YOUR BREATH :

We are always breathing. The breath is life itself. Do all the prep that was previously described, and get very comfortable. Again, comfort is key for seated meditation. You want to find a place where you are not thinking about your body, but feeling your body with ease. Sit with your eyes closed and just follow and feel your breath. Tell your mind, "Okay mind, I know you have the ability to focus, now focus on my breath." Follow your inhalation from bottom to top, follow your exhalation from top to bottom. Focus more on your exhalations and let the inhalations happen on their own with little to no effort. Like clouds floating in the sky, thoughts will come and thoughts will go. Practice observing the thought and sensation the moment they arise. Label thoughts as "thinking" and sensations as just "sensations," and let them go. Neither push your experience away, nor grab onto it or make it you. Be in the middle path. Just observe. Sit and feel your breath as you inhale and exhale. Be gentle with your breath. You can inhale and exhale through your nose only, or inhale through your nose and exhale through your mouth. Over time, gently allow your breath to deepen. Relax your belly, relax your face, jaw, and eyes. Ignore the thoughts and feel your breath. If the mind wanders again, come back to your breath. Repeat this practice of watching when you get absorbed with thought, and bring your awareness back to your breath without judgment, or labeling it as "good" or "bad." When you can get out of your head and stop identifying with thoughts, you are riding the wave of ecstasy and bliss in your Now, which is always present. Although you're not paying attention to it most of the time, now you are!

Sit and breathe for however long you set your timer, and see what happens. Try not to quit early. Stay with it. When it gets boring and you really want to stop and move, this is a powerful moment of transformation. Notice when you feel an itch on your nose and resist the temptation to scratch it. Be still. This is very important, especially if you are new to this practice. Your mind will want to quit right away. Remember to set a realistic time to sit. Longer is not better by any means. Trust me! Back to your breathe. You can make a game with yourself of counting to 10. An inhale and exhale equals one. Inhale and exhale again, is two. Count your breath cycle until you get to 10, then repeat. If a thought comes into your mind during the counting, label it as a "thought" and start at one again. See if you can expand the space between thoughts from 1 to 10, only focusing on your breath. You may only get to two and then think a thought, that's okay. Start again, and again, and again. You have your entire life to practice this. When you get to 10, nothing happens. You get nothing physical, however you are training your mind to be calm and creating space between your thoughts.

It is in the space between thought where we can live our lives in pure awareness and devotion to our passions. If the mind wanders, go back to your breath. Mind wanders, back to the breath. It's really a fun game if you can laugh at yourself and not take it all too seriously. What a gift to have a human body, to breathe, and have the clarity to observe your mind and body in such a powerful, mindful way. Wow, we are blessed. Smile, for life is so damn good! From this training you learn to be aware of your thoughts, and use them as tools to create your existence on Earth. You deliberately use your thoughts to create, as the creator that you are. What a gift!

: SITTING WITH WHAT IS :

First, do the preparation described for all the meditation practices. Now set yourself up to sit, and then just sit. There is no technique and no goal with this practice. No desire to an outcome. No process. Just sit as still and straight as you can while observing everything that is happening within and without you. Just be there in that moment, with no attachment to what happens. Watch what happens. Don't think about what is happening, just watch as if you were watching a fascinating movie. If your mind becomes to cluttered or overwhelmed, focus on your breathing or any other repetitive sound. This is a very powerful and transformative practice. Watch the world around you move and vibrate while feeling the aliveness of your inner body. Notice that you don't even need to do anything.

Your body functions and lives without you needing to do or think one damn thing. When a woman gets pregnant, she is not given a manual on how she needs to think and function internally to make the baby. Certain thoughts and actions can help, but her body just makes a baby! It's amazing! This is the same with everyday living. Your body will work perfectly in all ways if you allow it to just be. The body will function with perfect health and healing as long as you are not getting in the way with unwanted thoughts, stories, and images.

Be very kind and playful with these meditation practices. If you are brand new to this way of thinking and you have never meditated before, go slow. Be easy and kind to yourself. It is important to make it a priority and a part of your life. Set a meditation schedule and a designated time to sit. If you want to reap the benefits of meditation, you must do this often! I suggest sitting for 15 minutes in the morning not long after you wake up, and 15 minutes before you go to bed. If that amount of time is too long at first, then shorten it. It is also important to sit for the entire time you originally intended. Do this for a while, maybe a month, maybe a year.

Eventually you will start to see shifts in your everyday life, internally and externally. You will know when it is time to add or subtract time, how often to sit, or change your routine. Don't make this a job or something you have to do. You must want this, especially since it is challenging. Your mind may say "no" but your heart and soul say "yes." Listen to your heart. For a while your mind will never really want to sit. It can think of a billion other things to do and is very good and manipulating you to follow this or that thought into action. That is all part of the process. Over time meditation is something you will want to do. You will do it whenever it feels natural, with no set schedule or time. It might be on the bus ride to school or work. It might be on an airplane. It might be while you're waiting for your food to cook or doing the dishes. Your whole life becomes a meditation! At first, try to follow your schedule as best as you can. Be kind and gentle with it. If you miss a day, don't stress about it. Do not treat it as a means to an end, for there is no end. The more you practice the easier it becomes, and the better you feel. Ready, set, sit!

: MINDFULNESS AND ALLOWING YOURSELF TO BE :

Most importantly, through meditation practice your entire waking life eventually becomes a meditation. We start seated, and from there everything we do becomes meditation: walking, talking, eating, driving, dancing, playing, sex. Everything! Because what we are doing in the seated practice is practicing mindfulness, which means to become fully aware of what we are doing internally and externally. It is awareness of your actions, thoughts, words, and the world around you. Mindful thinking, walking, running, cooking, reading, listening, talking, acting, observing. Mindful everything! Learning to be mindful is the goal of meditation. And mindfulness is different from concentration. Concentration implies effort. With mindfulness there is no effort, like a human child growing in the womb. The same goes for living our lives. We practice these meditations to live all of waking life mindfully, focusing purely on what you are doing in each moment. If you are talking to somebody, then you're fully engaged and present in that conversation, not thinking about work. If you notice when you are taking a shower or brushing your teeth, you are most likely thinking about something else like the past or the future. But can you be fully present with what is, moment to moment? Look at a tree and really see and feel it fully, no judgment, no labels. Just recognize the aliveness of that tree. Aaahhhhhh. You have the power to do, to have, or be whatever you want. Mindfulness is the key to living an exciting and blissful life. The moments when you notice you are not being present and mindful are just as important as when you are. For in the moment when you realize you are not present, you have instantly become present. Life is practice and there is no end to it. But you do get better and better, and can master all this. Even when you master it however, you are still practicing. It simply happens with more ease, grace, and compassion for yourself and all beings who are practicing this same game right alongside you. We are all in this together.

Think of something you are passionate about, whether it's sports, music, writing, cooking, parenting, or whatever. When are you doing what you love, you are physically and mentally in alignment with the present moment. In those moments you are not just thinking, but feeling. You are fully involved in it. It has your complete attention. All of life can be like this! I remember when I was younger, I was really into video games. I would spend hours immersed in the game I was playing. When you play a game you have to be totally in the moment, otherwise you will lose the game, yes? This applies to everything. The good news is that in this game of life you have infinite lives, you can't get anything wrong, and you can't ever lose! How fun! But you can lose sight of the beauty and the power of the moment and why you have come into this physical life experience. If you focus your life on whatever you love and are passionate about, it will be much easier to practice living life mindfully in the present moment. For when you are doing that which you love, you are not thinking, you are allowing. You are also not wishing you were doing something else. There is no guilt and no regret. It's fun to live this way. What are you waiting for? Put this book down for a moment, sit up straight, close your eyes, and take three slow deep breaths. Go ahead, I will wait here in the moment...

Feel a little more grounded? Present?

Life is waiting for you to open your arms and say "Yes! I'm here! I'm paying attention, and I'm ready for everything I have decided to manifest in this lifetime!" This is the life you have been dreaming of and waiting for! This is heaven, this is your vacation! Now is the time to live the life you deserve!

Trust yourself, you got this. Everything always works out for you, it does. Think about it. Be easy with everything I am saying. Don't overthink anything. Be playful, be easy. Be easy. Be easy. Have lightness in your life, don't take things so seriously. Don't feel like you need to control everything and everyone. Just focus on you and your inner peace, your inner well being. Let everything be. Let your body be. Let your family and friends be. Let the government be. Let your nation be. Let everything be. Let the Earth be. Let it be! Expect that everything will work out for you. Your whole life becomes a meditation.

Meditation is a homecoming. It is coming back inside, back to the Source that is you. You don't need to go anywhere. You don't have to go to India. You don't have to wear the beads, or look a certain way. You don't have to do yoga poses if you don't want to. You don't have to find a guru. You can do any of these things and they are all beautiful and powerful. What I am saying is that everything you are searching for is inside yourself. It always has been and always will be. You don't have to look or act a certain way in order to meditate and be spiritual. Start right here, where you are, as you are. Have fun with all this. This practice may come and go throughout your life. You might meditate every day for years. Sometimes not at all, and that's fine. There is no right or wrong. Listen to your body and heart, and trust your impulses on what to do and when to do it. All is good. Enjoy.

: 9 :

WHAT IT MEANS TO LIVE A SPIRITUAL & ENLIGHTENED LIFE

Being spiritual does not mean that you you have to grow a beard, eat vegan, do yoga, meditate for hours everyday, or go East and live with holy people. You can do all this if you are called, but you don't have to! It doesn't matter. Being a spiritual person means living life fully conscious and connected to the Now, with compassion and love for yourself, others, and everything on the planet. It means being yourself, your true self. You are the most important person in the universe, and when you feel good and at peace within yourself, then from the perspective of Source all is right within the universe. It's really that simple, my friends. Be yourself. Do what you love. Feel good. Live mindfully in unconditional alignment, love, and clarity as best as humanly possible. You can be a hardcore goth in a Satanic black metal band and still be spiritual. You can live anywhere in the world and be into anything, and if you are doing so authentically and mindfully with love in your heart and clarity in your mind then you are just as spiritual as the Dalai Lama. Being spiritual means you know and trust that everything is always working out for you and everyone else. You know that you can have, do, or be anything you desire in this lifetime. You know that joy and peace are the foundation of what it means to be human. You know that you are here to have a good time on Earth and that you have a team of guides, masters, and healers that are always by your side every step of the way. You know you are an eternal, powerful, divine, Creator-God!

I used to frequent a goth nightclub in Chicago called Neo. I went there on and off for many years. I would always see the same man, dancing in the same spot every single time. He always wore a white shirt and black pants. Every time I was there, he was there. He was always so happy. He would dance to every song that played. He appeared to give himself fully to the moment and dance his heart out. There seemed to be no judgment of the music that was playing, nor did he care who was around him. He would dance for hours just being himself completely, while surrendering to the moment and having the time of his life. If you watched him closely, you could tell that his body was there dancing in alignment with the fullness that he is. He was totally in alignment with his true self and Source energy. Pure golden white light radiated from him. He never danced with anyone, nor payed attention to other people. Now I realize that he was dancing with God. This was his spiritual practice. When you're doing your craft, living out your passion in the moment, then you're truly grounded in your body and blissed out with Source energy. You are fully aligned and balanced with the essence of all that you are. We see this in athletes, musicians, actors, teachers, and artists of all kinds. You see, it does not matter what you are doing. It matters why you are doing it. If you do whatever you are doing with the fullness of who you are, present in the moment and with love in your heart, then you are spiritual. And Source is right there doing it with you and through you. It can be washing the dishes, exercising, meditating, walking, reading... anything.

Some people think that being spiritual is some higher state of super-humanness. Or that it entails going to another plane of existence, transcending to someplace else, or becoming a "larger than life" person. I don't believe this to be so. Being spiritual is realizing that being mindfully in alignment with Source energy is superhuman, and naturally brings you to higher states of consciousness and aliveness! You don't have to try and reach any state, or go somewhere. Spirituality is available right here, right now, all the time, on this Earth. You always have super human powers! You just forget about them! Return to Chapter 7 and the "what about me" trip if you need a reminder. Other people make you think you are powerless and hopeless, which is the furthest thing from the truth. You aren't going anywhere when you're spiritual or enlightened. You're coming back home. It is an elevated state of consciousness and deep awareness of yourself and everything and everyone around you. Children are naturally in this state unless conditioned not to be. Spirituality is about being fully human on Earth and enjoying everything through your senses, while at the same time expanding your consciousness by going beyond your senses, deep into your inner world. You are realizing what has been forgotten, which is how to be totally alive and mindful on this planet. If you were meant to be on another planet in another galaxy, then you would be there. But if you're reading this book, you are like me and you are of this Earth. Being spiritual or enlightened does not dehumanize us, it maximizes our humanness. You're still you. You're just more aware of God, your mind, your guides, and all the non-physical energy out there waiting to assist you in gaining clarity, wisdom, healing, and growth. You become more aware of what you are doing and why you are doing it day-to-day, moment to moment. No more auto pilot. You are not attaining a higher state outside of your body. You are using your body and mind to experience all that this life has to offer. Life is whatever you choose it to be.

You don't get superhuman powers, you already have them. You don't create deep states of clarity and vitally, you already have them within you. You wake up to the power that has always been within since birth! You are remembering what you knew to be true before you came into this body! What you knew as a baby, and what you knew as a young child. Enlightenment and being spiritual, is waking up from the dream of illusion, fear, and ignorance, and returning to who you really are. The energy that is available to you from non-physical beings is limitless. All who have come before us, all the Gods and Goddesses, saints and sages, angels, animal guides, and previous masters are still here, wanting to be with you and assist you with whatever you need. All you need to do is allow everything to be as it is. And you get into a state of allowing by feeling good emotionally. Remember whenever you feel alone that we are all in this together, and you are never truly alone. We are always guided and protected, especially when we are in alignment with Source energy and the wholeness of who we are.

Now, more on this enlightenment topic. You might still be wondering what is it and how you get there. First, there is no "there." It's already right here, in the present moment. This is why living in the Now is so important. Not in the future nor the past, just now. Enlightenment happens Now, within your body and heart. Enlightenment is feeling unconditional alignment with Source energy in everything you do in your Now. You don't need external conditions to change in order to feel this alignment. Your mind is clear, and you focus on feeling the fullness of who you are with pure love in your heart. You have a stable mind through all the ups and downs of emotional life without identifying with everything you experience internally and externally. You maintain this sense of steady grounded clarity no matter what happens around you or within you. You can ride the wave of life and not be completely thrown off your boat. It means being able to consciously and deliberately create your own existence. You are totally involved with life while not allowing what happens to dominate your inner peace and clarity. You care about things and people, but things and people do not rule who you are and how you feel.

It is also important to note that feeling awakened and enlightened is not a destination. It's not something you experience once, and then feel it now and forever more. It's not like you can obtain a college degree in Enlightenment, and then it's yours permanently. Sorry folks, it is up to you to keep stirring the nectar of love and grace and alignment within your heart. The feeling comes and goes. The intensity of the feeling comes in waves. Imagine enlightenment, which again is alignment with Source energy in your body, as a flower seed. Choose a flower, whatever your favorite flower is. The seed of enlightenment needs your daily spiritual practice to blissfully water and tend to it until it grows into a flower. You keep watering the flower to keep it alive. You have to keep doing your spiritual practice, or you will forget about enlightenment and it disappears. Fortunately, you can plant another seed and blossom another flower quickly. But you must keep tending to it everyday, every moment. You do this by living life mindfully with awareness and love in your heart. You do this by meditating every morning. You do this by practicing yoga daily, if that is your practice. You do this by following and living out your dreams and passions. You do this by being your true self as best as you can, everyday. It is very easy to forget about your spiritual practice. It is very easy to lose the feeling of alignment and let the flower die. The good news is that it's much easier to get back on track and plant another seed once you have started! All you have to do is choose to feel good. Sit and meditate again for 15 minutes. Roll out your yoga mat. Clean the house. Go out into nature. Love your pet. Sing a song. Dance like nobody's watching. When you're feeling good, you're there. When you're not feeling so good that means you have stopped tending to your flower. So be aware of that, and with appreciation start taking care of it again.

Keep watering the plant, or plant a new one. You have endless plants, and endless water. Don't get caught up with all the distractions that keep you from watering the plant. Create balance in your life and stay on course. Enjoy all this. You have your entire life to practice everything in this book and I highly suggest you start now. Don't wait for the perfect moment because it never comes. Don't wait until you're old and retired. Don't wait until you're on vacation. Start now! Now, Now, Now! If you are reading this book, that means you're ready to start some or all of these teachings. Do a little watering here, a little watering there. Don't do any of this to achieve a certain state or get anything physical. Set intentions and trust the process. Want things, but don't do any of these processes or practices to attain anything other than alignment with your inner being of Source energy. Do all this because coming into alignment is fun! Do it for the joy of knowing that you deliberately went from not feeling so good, to then feeling good! Do this simply to experience feeling good, and when you do all will come. I promise you this. Everything comes when you are in the state of feeling good.

How beautiful is this Earth? How delicious is making love to somebody you deeply care about? What is that feeling you feel when you have an amazing orgasm? Or the feeling you get when you listen to a beautiful piece of music that touches your soul and gives you goosebumps? What is that feeling of pure appreciation in the moment? What are these feelings? It's not thought. It's not words. It's you aligning with the wholeness of who you are and to Source energy, and then doing that which brings you joy and pleasure.

: INVOKE THE MASTER :

Most people need to be taught how to live life mindfully, to meditate, practice yoga asana, and create and live out their spiritual life. It is similar to learning how to sing, or play a sport, or master any other skill. Some people need to be told that they are living the "what about me" trip.

114

If you grew up isolated from the world, and the only people you know are those who live in your town, your friends, and your church, then you may not even know that there is another way to live. You might not even know what enlightenment is. You might not know that you are more than your thoughts or your body. The Buddha taught that ignorance is a major cause of suffering. Many people need to be told about or taught the practices I am offering to you. These days the internet makes it easier to start the awakening process on your own. But in the beginning, mostly everyone needs a guru.

A guru is a teacher or master. A guru is someone who brings you out of the darkness and into the light. He or she assists you on your path to awakening. They tell you what to do and give you a map! If possible, find someone who lives in your country, state or town who has mastered whatever you want to learn or master yourself. If it is yoga asana, find a master of yoga asana who you can connect with face-to-face. The same person who helped you with your deep dark work can also assist you with what you want learn or master. You may have many gurus throughout your life. They come and go as you need them. The guru finds you. You get whoever and whatever you need in perfect timing. So it is important to study with someone you feel deeply connected to. If when you see them, and every cell in your body tells you this is the right person to be your guru, then listen to that instinct and follow it. Even if you need to leave your hometown, or travel to be with this person. Do whatever is needed. What you put into your spiritual practice is what you get out of it. You have to go all the way. You have to love them. The guru is love and will love you unconditionally from the inside out. They should not ask you for money in exchange for some mantra or sacred practice guaranteed to enlighten. The guru should not say they are your only way and hope to God. The guru is pure love and will do whatever is needed for you to bathe completely in that same love free of charge. How do you find this guru? Ask the universe to bring you to together, and stay alert. They will find you in perfect timing. When you find them it may be in a form of a picture, or song, or movie. Every cell in your body will know. In that moment, you will feel pure love and the need to be with them. There will be no questions asked and no doubt in your mind. These feelings are your inner guidance system telling you to act.

Look to the masters, teachers, gurus, saints, and sublime sages of this Earth, who are either still alive or have left their bodies. They could be from any culture, time, or space. Anyone. If you want to be the best version of whatever you want to be, then find someone who is doing or has done it. Find someone who inspires and motivates you to learn and grow. This goes for non-spiritual things as well. Whatever your job or passion is, find a master of the trade and do the same with them that you would with your spiritual guru. If you want to be the best body piercer you can be, find and spend as much time with someone who has mastered body piercing. If you want to be the best tennis player, find a tennis master and study with them as much as possible. Do you get what I am saying? Again, if you have to travel or relocate for a while, do so! It is very powerful to be in the presence of past or present masters. It invokes the master within you. They help ignite the flame and power that is already within you, to master the same thing the guru has mastered. If they can do it, you can do it. The master was once a student. Remember that!

If you can't physically be with a master, try YouTube, Facebook or other social media, books, movies, and the internet to study them, admire them, or just plain love them unconditionally. Throughout my life I have been interested in a variety of things. I wanted to be a professional D.J. so I listened to, watched, and studied other D.J.s. I did the same when I wanted to be an artist, a rock star, a body piercer, a tattoo artist, a yoga teacher, a real estate agent, and a hair stylist. Yes, at one point I wanted to be all these things. And you know what? In every field of interest, I found someone who taught me how to be the best version of myself in whatever I wanted to do. This includes my spiritual practice. I continue to study the masters of Hatha yoga, meditation, mindfulness, kirtan, Bhakti yoga, Nada Yoga, magic, the Christ and Buddha energy, and so on. I pay attention to people, alive or not, who are doing or have done what I want to do or be. I have practiced their teachings and studied their lives. I learn from them in person as much as possible, or I use books and the internet. There are some masters that I love with all of my heart, who I do not study but just keep their pictures around in order to always be in the energy of pure love. Some gurus and masters I just love, praise and appreciate. Others I appreciate, as well as study and learn from them. The ones I truly just love are teaching me how to love unconditionally. It is important to have a positive influence in your life, someone to look up to and give you the hope that it is possible to reach your full potential and more. Find someone in this way with regard to your spiritual life and practices, including your job, passions, hobbies, and so on.

Who do you look up to? Who do you praise and consider a master of their trade, or passion? Talk about those people. Think about those people. Bow down to pictures of them on your altar. Give thanks and praise to them. By doing so you radiate their wisdom and power within yourself. It can be anyone in any pursuit in the world, not just spiritual. If you want to be the best basketball player in the world, you can admire Michael Jordan or any other player you look up to. Again, it has to be personal to you. As you study and admire these masters, do so without losing yourself or comparing yourself to them. Don't lose your worth and values or the core of who you are. Don't compare their journey to yours. Let them inspire you and motivate you to greatness! The masters are the same as you, human. Buddha and Jesus were humans just like you and me. They just gave themselves fully to their goals and desires. Michael Jordan made it his main goal to be the best basketball player ever, and he was because he never let go of that goal. His clear focus on what he wanted gave him the power and skill to rise to the top. He's not superhuman. He found out how to be fully human. Being fully human makes you super powerful! That's big! Mike was clear and unwavering with his intention and believed with every cell of his body that he can be, do, or have anything. The same goes for you, my brothers and sisters. Masters devote their lives to finding their truth and remaining consistently in alignment with Source energy as much as possible. They created their own customized spiritual path. If their path is similar to your path or journey, that's great. Maybe you also want to be the best basketball player, but you still have to customize it to your wants, needs and lifestyle. So many people blindly follow a path that has been laid out for them and don't question any of it. They call it their religion or spiritual practice. Christianity is an example. They say, "Here's the Bible. Everything in it is true and not to be questioned. You must follow it and believe in all of it. If you don't, you will be punished." I am not bashing Christianity, religions or any other belief system, only using it as an example. If something from the Bible resonates within you, then take it to heart.

Do what makes you happy. Don't make other people's religions or spiritual practice your path to the Truth. See other paths as inspiration to create your own sacred fire within. Pick and choose from other religions or practices that connect to your own heart and soul, and make them your own. That's what I do. Be your true self. You may be faced with the expectations of others, say those of your family or other social groups for example. But it is important to listen to yourself and what feels true to you. If you just want to master being a good person, and if your dad is a good person who you look up to, then he can be your master, teacher, or main influence. Use whatever word you like. I like the word "master" because it entails countless hours of failing and succeeding at something you are passionate about. It means you have focused your energy on the topic so much that you, and the Source within you, can resonate with the joy of being it completely. By being your true self, you ignite the flame of the master that you already have within yourself. If they can do it, you can do it. Whatever you pay attention to, you attract and manifest in your life. As you focus on what you want, don't forget to be your authentic self. Don't lose yourself. I feel the need to repeat this because I have done this myself. I have tried to be the person that I admire. I have identified with some person and tried to imitate them, rather than just being Mahkah.

Stay true to what you know to be your Truth. Believe only what resonates within your own heart and soul. Make it yours and have fun with it. There are so many things to enjoy. So many awesome people have walked on this planet. So much knowledge and mastery is out there for us to use and have fun with. We are here to enjoy everything under the sun. I want you to be the best you can be at whatever you are passionate about. We all want to be something. Realize what that is and find inspiration and guidance from the masters. Make it your main intention to be yourself, and let the rest go. Forget about what the world wants you to be and just be you, my friend. Find a spiritual guru of what you want to master, who you can interact with and relate to. Make it as general or specific as you like. You can have Buddha on your altar or another Lama, an engineer, an athlete, Bruce Lee, Krishna or Anandamayi Ma, or all of them. Make it personal and customized! This is the way to becoming your own master and guru. Then perhaps you can be a guru and master for others.

: 10 :

EVERYTHING IS RELATIONSHIP

Everything we do on Earth involves creating relationships, whether they are with ourselves, our emotions, other humans, animals, nature, and with Ma. We want healthy, balanced relationships in our lives. There is a beautiful quote from the movie Into The Wild based on the life of Christopher McCandless. Just before his death he wrote, "Happiness is only real when shared." Life is meant to be shared with other people. We are truly here to co-create together. A balanced life means having a healthy mental, physical and spiritual connection to ourselves, others, and with nature.

You may have heard the stories of yogis in the East, who retreat to the mountains and meditate in caves for years to attain enlightenment, yes? I have personally chosen that path many times in my past lives. So I understand that this kind of practice is sometimes needed to realize the truth of yourself. But, you don't have to go into the mountains and meditate all day long. Perhaps try a week-long silent meditation retreat at a spiritual center. Or make a commitment to meditate 15 minutes every morning for three months. Again, you must customize this journey to your wants, needs, conditions.

Back to the quote from Chris, life is ultimately to be shared and enjoyed with other people and to create with one another. It's about finding a balance of going within and aligning with Source energy while releasing resistance in solitude. Then you project outward into the world and teach what you have learned. It's called "the middle path" in Buddhism. You first go deep within, and from a state of total self-awareness and alignment with Source you go back out and live your life with others. The Buddha went through this. When the Buddha was a sadhu, he barely ate anything and meditated night and day. He purposefully put himself through hell and back to understand the reason for suffering, and to find enlightenment. As the story goes, one day during his meditation the Buddha was listening to an old music teacher talking to his student. The music teacher said to his student, "If you tighten the string too much it will snap, and if you leave it too slack it won't play." Think about that one! How true is that? Life and all relationships are about balance. Too much or little of anything throws us off balance and creates disharmony in the mind and body. Over time this creates sickness and suffering.

: FINDING A BALANCED RELATIONSHIP WITH EARTH MOTHER AND SKY FATHER :

Creating relationships is the most important part of our existence on Earth. The Law of Attraction will bring you more of whatever you pay attention to, wanted or unwanted.

The Law of Attraction will also bring you people who match your vibration. You become who you surround yourself with. Creating healthy relationships is just this: you create them based on the dominant vibration you broadcast. You also become what you see, hear, eat and drink. By living life you specify what you do and do not want day-to-day, moment to moment. For example, if you frequently focus on your former abusive relationship and remember how much she or he hurt you, your next partner will be the same or probably worse. If you are always worried about your body, you will attract other people worried about their bodies. If you are feeling happy and alive most of the time, you will attract other happy people. Get it? Let the relationship with yourself be the only relationship that truly matters. When you do, you will resonate and align with your inner being, resulting with you feeling good and attracting others who feel this way too. You will attract other people with a similar vibration. This is how everything works. Like attracts like. Feel good and the people you want in your life will come, and the ones you don't want around will have to leave. Creating healthy, sacred relationships with others begins with creating and maintaining a healthy relationship to yourself throughout your life. Tend to the relationship with yourself by creating your spiritual practice and doing your deep dark work, while enjoying everyday life as much as possible.

Another important relationship is the one we have with this beautiful, sacred Earth. Our bodies evolved from this Earth, not another planet. Aliens are not producing us on other planets and then dropping us off here. We come from Earth Mother. We breathe the air of this Earth, which is also part of the universe. We breath in air, parts of which may come from other galaxies! Breath is the life of all living things. Creating a deep relationship with Earth Mother is important to finding balance in your body, mind and spirit, and for your healing and growth on all levels. So let's talk about finding this balance between Earth Mother and Sky Father. The balance of being grounded here on Earth, feeling pleasure and creating through the senses, while also opening the mind to receiving wisdom and pleasure from the universe.

Creating balance in every avenue of life is paramount. The hatha yoga practice is all about balancing our bodies and minds, and creating union with universal Source energy. We must balance out the yin and the yang, light and dark, sun energy and moon energy, masculine and feminine, Shiva and Shakti. When we feel alive, frisky and in the flow, we are in balance. When we are sick or depressed, we are out of balance. Nature is magical and beautiful, just like you. We are nature. We are the Earth, the sky, and the stars. We are the space in the universe. When you are in balance with Earth Mother, Sky Father, and your inner being, you want to be outside and spend time in nature. You want to go on hikes, camping trips, and festivals. When you are in balance nobody needs to tell you to be a good person, to be peaceful and compassionate with your neighbor. You intuitively know all this, You just forget sometimes. You are a primal animal just like the rest of the beasts on this planet. But we humans are special because we have been given the gift of our senses and consciousness to experience the deliciousness of life and everything in it. The energy that creates worlds is you, within you and in all living things. Animals and nature hold this space of pure, unconditionally positive Source energy, unless someone trains them otherwise. You can teach an animal to hate, just like a human. But you don't have to train an animal or a human child to love.

The next time you are outside and see a tree, do this: walk up to the tree slowly and take a few deep, gentle breaths. Say hello. Use your senses to experience the aliveness and beauty of the tree. Touch it. Talk to it. Tell her how much you love her. Look at how beautiful she is. Place your hands on this tree and breathe with her. Feel the love she is giving back to you. It's alive and at peace and ease. Learn from her, listen, what is she telling you? You too can experience this same aliveness and calmness as the tree, but on a deeper, more pleasurable level.

I will now share one of my own experiences with nature and the elements, when I felt alive and in alignment with Source and the present moment. It was at Burning Man 2011. Burning Man is a gathering of 70,000+ people from around the world who come together for a week to celebrate art, radical self-expression, community, love, and life. Those who attend Burning Man create a massive city called Black Rock City in the middle of the Nevada desert. People build a massive wooden man and a city forms around it. It's one of the most magical places I have ever been. Saturday is the night when the man is burned. At nightfall everyone in the city gathers around the wooden effigy and dances, plays music, and spins fire in celebration. As the wooden man burns it eventually falls down to the ground of this ancient, sacred dried-up lakebed, and everyone runs or walks around the huge mound of sacred firewood. To give more context I was completely sober, and had nothing in my body besides pure food, water, and dust. There was nothing around me but the stars, moon, mountains, beautiful people, dust, the massive fire, and Earth Mother and Sky Father. Around the fire I noticed many people were naked, running and dancing around the fire like primal wild animals. My friend and I of course decided to join. I proceeded to dance and scream like an animal and completely let loose and wild. I was totally present and in alignment with Source in that moment. I was mentally and physically naked. I had no thoughts, and felt more alive and grounded than ever. Pure ecstasy and bliss coursed through my body and mind. I was fully connected to Earth Mother and Sky Father with no barriers between us because my mind was clear. I was dancing and playing with other people who were also being who they were. No masks, no fake fronts. Pure humans acting like the animals that we are. Before that day I never felt such power and connection to nature. It was so much fun! Days later, I reflected that this was a feeling I wanted to experience all the time.

So you see we need some sort of connection to the Earth in our everyday lives. By creating a balanced relationship with Earth Mother and Sky Father, we come directly into alignment with the wholeness of who we truly are. You have to be able to get naked, maybe literally, and get out of your way to fully connect with nature. This happens easily when you have done your deep dark work and have a meditation practice. When the mind's clutter and chatter fades away you can experience a rich, deep connection with nature and other people.

Many in the west and around the world have lost this connection. They live a life confined within walls. They go to sleep in a bed, inside a house. Get into some sort of a transport to go to work. Work is probably inside for most, sometimes without any windows. After work they get back into the transport, back to their walled house, and back to a bed. Not everyone does this but the majority of the world does. Where is the connection to nature? As I write this, I am living in Portland Oregon. I have noticed how nice, caring, and respectful people are here. The pace of the city and its people is easy and calm. Most people don't seem to be in a rush. They look out for one another. People smile and truly care when they ask you, "How are you today?" I feel one reason for this is because Portlanders make time to connect to the Earth on a regular basis. Nature in the Pacific Northwest is intoxicating. The nature here is abundant and breathtakingly beautiful. It makes it easier to connect to when nature is so accessible. Chicago, where I grew up, is a much harsher, rough and fast-paced city. Many people seem to be in a rush to get from one place to the next. There is not much nature there, and miles of big buildings. I love Chicago dearly and always will. Again, everything is about balance and perspective. Too much or little of one thing creates imbalance, whether that is the physical walls of a room or walls created in the mind. If you look at the indigenous people of Earth, they have been living completely off of the land since the beginning of time. There are some tribes that have never had contact with the outside world and are mostly thriving. They live life connected to Spirit and to the Earth. This is because the Earth provides us with everything we need to thrive and create life.

Take time to go outside, look around, and connect with the Mother. Pay attention to how you feel when you are in nature. Walk around barefoot in your backyard and feel the energy of the Mother radiate through your body. She is here to heal us, and help us grow and expand. Go on more camping trips. If you ever feel confused about something in your life go on a camping trip alone. That will give you some clarity, I promise. Get out there and embrace this beautiful world. Make it a priority to connect with nature. It helps to bring your body and mind into balance and alignment with the wholeness of all that you are. It can help you find clarity as to why you have come into this physical life experience, or on any topic you desire. You will feel more alive and connected to the wholeness of not just you, but of life and everybody here riding this wave with you. Go create a sacred relationship with nature and you will start to feel good, better than you do now. And remember, that is what you truly want. To feel good and have fun.

The relationship we have with food is also important. All pure and healthy food comes from the Earth. Be mindful of what you put into your body. If you eat something and it makes you feel tired, bloated, and like crap then it's probably something that does not work for your highest healing and growth. Try eating more plant-based foods that come straight from the Earth, and have not been modified or tampered with. Eating animals is good for some for they also come from the Earth. If you eat meat, try to eat the most pure, organic, and humanely-raised meat you can find. The energy of the animal's life stays in the meat after it is killed. All food and water is energy and holds vibration. If the animal lived a life of suffering, that negative energy stays in the meat. You then consume that negative energy into your body temple and it becomes you. That's why I always give thanks, bless, and purify my food before I eat it. I turn the food into pure love light energy before it goes into my body. I make it sacred. I believe this works, so it works. The food is sanctified for my highest healing and growth.

This all comes down to living a mindful, conscious life. Eating, talking, meditating, everything becomes a sacred practice. And we do this again and again because we want to feel good. So do what you do mindfully, and live it up! Listen to your body. Listen to your emotional guidance system. Listen to your gut. It will never misguide you. I promise. Now go outside and hug a tree!

: 11 :

THE DIFFERENT LEVELS OF SELF REALIZATION

When it comes to interacting with other humans we tend to have different levels of self that we portray depending on the social situation we are in. For instance, you might act differently at work than you do with your lover. You act one way on a first date, and another way on your honeymoon. You will act a certain way on a bus than you would in a car full of friends, yes? What are we actually doing? My theory is that we have three levels of self. They are: our best self, our true self, and our shadow self. You can think of these three selves as masks that you wear around certain people or situations. If you have seen The Mask, you can think of them as the mask in the movie. The mask affects everyone differently depending on their personal life situations, moods, and how much deep dark work they have done.

The first self I mentioned is our best self. The best self is the one we wear on a first date, a job interview, or out in public. It's the self you show when you are feeling bad inside, but have to work that day at the hair salon so you pretend to be happy. You might be feeling very angry at someone, but when you're with them you pretend everything is fine. It's the mask of covering up some part of the truth that you don't want others to see. Most of the time, the best self hides the deep dark work that has not been addressed. This mask keeps all the demons inside locked in their proper cages. The best self is an aspect of who you are, however it may not be a true reflection of how you might be feeling inside. You usually put this mask on consciously. It brings you a sense of security and comfort. It's the the best version of you, even if it's not even close to the core of who you are in that moment. It is the person you genuinely wish you really were all the time, even if you feel differently. You feel down and out, but you want to feel happy and alive. So this mask is the mask of happy and alive, but it's really an illusion. It simply covers up how you really feel inside, when what you truly want is for the outside to reflect what is on the inside. When your thoughts, words, and actions align seamlessly, you create another form of enlightenment.

The true self is the one that emerges when you are alone in your room at night or when you are with people you love. It's the self we want to be all time, when we are acting and speaking our truth. When you don't feel good, this is the self you reach for. This mask completely matches what you feel inside. It is God meeting God, with no fakeness or fronts. It's the self you wear when you are doing deep healing and spiritual work as the healer of the one being healed. It's the self that feels alive and vital when you're having fun and feeling good, when you're in the moment and doing what you love to do. It's the mask that tells the truth and sees the truth clearly. It's the self that is compassionate and loving to all living beings. It's in alignment with Source energy through your body. This is the self that you can always be wearing once the deep dark work is done, and you are totally confident and comfortable in your own body and mind. It's the self that dominates when you are in a state of enlightenment. In time you can wear this mask almost permanently, seldom taking it off. It might fall off here and there, but you can quickly and easily put it back on. You might mindfully switch masks for a specific occasions, but you are aware of this and can switch back as you desire with ease and grace.

And finally, our shadow self. This is the self that identifies and relates with all the deep dark feelings of past trauma, abuse, and negative or unpleasant memories and experiences from your life. This is the part of you that is in pain and screaming for you to pay attention. When this mask is on it brings up the deep dark inner work that has been ignored or pushed away. This mask is on when you are heavily intoxicated, when you are alone or with the people you love. You never really want to wear this mask. You want to keep it hidden from others, in a box under the bed and bolted with a heavy duty lock. However this self really wants out of the box, to be realized and worked on. That's why it comes out. When this mask is worn it's like an update reminder on your phone. The negative emotions, memories, and thoughts are waving their hands, saying, "Hello! I'm here and you know it. I'm ready to be worked on, healed, and let go!" When this shadow self runs your life, when it is not healed and released, it can control your life completely. It is tied to stress and depression. When this mask is on for long periods of time, with no attention to healing work it can make people take their own lives, or destroy relationships. We always have a shadow self, but it becomes smaller the more work you do. It goes from controlling your life, to just another thing that has come to the surface that needs some healing. You can become aware of when the mask comes on, and not freak out when it does because you know what it means and what to do. This is why the mindfulness practice is so important. You notice the mask is on, and then right away you do something about it with grace and ease. You don't get mad at yourself when this mask comes on. You do your work and move on. No big deal. It requires work to live in this state of mind. The work is everything I have already suggested. Again, everything in this book is related and part of the same tree.

The shadow self appears when you get into a fight with your lover. You may be fighting about him or her not paying enough attention to you, but really it stems back to something deeper and more intimate from childhood or a past life. The self you want to ignore and hide from others and yourself is the self you have to work on sooner or later. The following section describes the dynamic of all three selves in an intimate relationship situation between two people who have not done their deep dark work. Pay attention because this is a wild ride!

Let's say you are single. Then you meet someone you like. You go on your first date. You put on your best clothes and your best self, and so does the other person. The date goes very well. Your best self likes the other person's best self. You go on a second date, still wearing the mask of your best self with glimpses of your true self beginning to show. After some time you become more comfortable with this person's best self only. When you finally have sex, your true self maybe comes out and you put your best self aside for a while. You don't think about your shadow self at all in that moment. Before or after the sexual experience you make the relationship official, but you still only know this person's best self with a little of the true self and shadow self showing up. A few months go by, maybe years, and you're still primarily putting your best self on for this person. Your true self will, of course, come out on occasion. However your shadow self remains mostly hidden from the other person, consciously or unconsciously.

An intimate relationship has been created where you both are dating each other's best selves. You allow your true self to come out here and there, but the mask of your best self is still the dominant one. You are afraid, and rightfully so, to show your partner your full shadow self. This cycle can go on for months, or even years, of living and sharing a life with each other. Time goes by and you start to see glimpses of each other's shadow self through arguments, fights, and unpleasant life circumstances. You now live with each other, or you might be married with kids, and you are still suppressing the shadow self in fear of your partner seeing it, not liking it, and leaving you. One day you get into a fight, or a friend or family member dies, or you become really intoxicated, or something negative happens in your life and your shadow self comes out! The mask is on with no filters. A volcano just erupted! Your partner, now witnessing your shadow self in full form, says, "Wow, I have never seen this side of you before, and I don't like it! Who is this person? What is going on? Who did I marry/move in/have kids with?" Now everyone freaks the fuck out and the other person's shadow self is probably triggered. A full-fledged meltdown happens. You see a side of the person you had no idea even existed. You don't like this "new" person and would have never dated them if you knew then what you know now. So everything gets ugly and you separate or divorce, or someone cheats, or you abuse each other. If you don't do your deep dark shadow work, you just end up repeating this process with your next three husbands or wives and call it bad luck. The end.

Did you follow all that? People form relationships with their best selves and true selves. The shadow self hides until it can't be hidden anymore. One day it comes out and it can, though not always, destroy a relationship. This is a very general but common example. The success of a relationship depends on how much deep dark work each person involved has done on their shadow self. I know many people who have had this type of relationship, including myself. So this all goes back to doing your work. Not doing your work just for yourself now, but for everyone you will be in relationship with. This scenario can happen with your best friend, lover, business partner, or whoever is closest to you. You get this, yes? If not, read it again because it's big.

A healthy, mindful person has an awareness of these three selves and can balance them. He or she knows where each mask is stored and knows the moment they put one on. A healthy relationship is where both people involved are consciously doing their best to heal their deep dark work. Don't be afraid to let the monster out of the dark dungeon and do your shadow work. You and everyone around you will benefit. Everyone will always have something to work on, whether it be small or big. A healthy relationship is one in which the three selves are accepted, supported, and are able to coexist, including the shadow self. If you can love a person's best self, true self, and shadow self unconditionally, then that is someone worth spending your life with. That goes for a best friend, business partner, or lover.

: 12 :

LETTING GO & AWAKENING TO THE POWER YOU

Don't be afraid to go down rabbit hole of your soul and experience your fears and pains. Growing up in my parents house I was always afraid of the dark, especially our basement. When I was young, there was something about being in the dark and going down into that basement I found absolutely terrifying. I think a lot of people can relate to this. I now see that it wasn't the dark or the actual basement that I was afraid of. It was the darkness within the basement of my soul. The basement that held all my negative past experiences, emotions, and trauma from this lifetime and all the lives I have ever lived. Everything you have done in every life stays with you, good and bad. This is what the Buddha meant when he talked about karma. You are born again and again. That dark basement and everything in it follows you until the day you open the door and shine your light of love and healing and release the darkness hidden away in your soul. I have lived many lifetimes on this Earth and other planets. I have lived many dark lives. I have had many negative images and emotions come up for me from past lives that I have been blessed to work on and release in this lifetime. It was scary and intense work at times. But it was liberating when I actually did my deep dark work and released the pain and karma of my past lives. I immediately felt like a brand new man after completing a healing session. Version 3, 4, 5, 6, 7, 8, 9.0 and so on. Everything shifts in a positive way mentally, emotionally, and spiritually when the real work is done. That's how I knew it worked and is true.

The bliss and ecstasy of being alive and at ease in your body and mind is real and ready for you now. Get whatever help you need. Pay whoever you need to pay. Go where you need to go. You can maybe do this work on your own, but as I have said before many of us need the help of another. You can determine what you need by listening to your body. If you feel that you need help, you need help. Don't feel ashamed or defeated. Let go of your pride. Be humble! These days there are so many wonderful avenues to healing. Whatever you need will present itself to you when you get out of your way. When this work is done, the shadow self becomes smaller and shows up less frequently in your life and relationships.

Peace within yourself and in all of your relationships is possible. If I can do this, so can you. No matter how horrible or messed up you think you or your life is. There is peace, love, and freedom from this process that you will want. I promise you. Do your work, and let it go. No matter how bad your past has been, even if you murdered someone, you can heal and grow and align with the wholeness of who you are. There is no need to hold onto whatever is causing you pain and suffering. It is not who you are. Even if you have held onto this pain your entire life, it is okay to let it go. Get out of the way of your healing and growth. If you are aware of something negative in your life that won't go away on its own or by ignoring it, then it is time to see it clearly, heal it, learn from it, and let it go! Live this birth for all it's worth and experience all this life has to offer you. Become enlightened in this lifetime! Why wait for another? I can't stress it enough to be easy with all this. Play with it, and don't take yourself and your thoughts so seriously. Thoughts are just thoughts! Learn to use your brain when you want to, just like your feet. You walk when you decide to walk. Your feet don't control you and run around whenever they feel like it. The same goes for your mind and thoughts. You are the master! All is well. You've got this. Everything always works out for you, for me, for everyone. Everything always works out for you. Everything always works out for you. Everything always works out for you!

As I write this, I am looking out my window into my backyard in Portland Oregon. I can see a large black crow and a squirrel playing with each other. At first it seemed like they are fighting. But after watching them for several minutes I realize they are surely playing with each other. The squirrel and the crow are teasing and dancing around one another. There is no thought, no expectations, no goals, and no attachment to the outcome. They seem to be enjoying this dance and play of life. I cannot stop laughing because this is what life's all about! Their dance reflects so much of what I have been talking about. This life is a gift. You are meant to have fun and enjoy every moment of your life. Please give yourself a break and don't take everything so seriously. Yes, contrast comes, people die, you might get sick, you lose the big game or the important deal, or your partner breaks up with you. Life happens, but it's about how you react and identify with these events. Do you become the slave or the master?

You need contrast to clarify what you really want from knowing what you really don't want. In what ways do you let the world affect your mood or alter who you are? How much do you identify with the thoughts in your mind? How much do you let what happens disrupt your inner peace and clarity? Can you be clearly involved with whatever is happening right now, whether it be internal or external, and not let it take over who you are? Can you be totally blissed out without needing the external world to change? Yes!

We humans have been afraid to do the inner work that we know needs to be done. Even with all this technology and smart devices, we lose touch with what really matters and who we are. There are so many ways to distract ourselves from doing our inner work and enjoying the moment. That being said, it's also important to play with all these teachings. Don't overthink anything. Find the path of least resistance with everything in your life. Play more. Laugh at yourself more. Become more humble every day. See the simplicity and humor in everything within and around you, especially your mind and thoughts. Maintain childlike awareness to whatever is happening in the present moment. Stop trying so hard. Stop beating yourself up. Stop trying to figure everything out. Stop trying to make things happen. Stop trying to plan out every future event and trying to make it perfect. Stop worrying, and stop fighting with people and the world. All is good for you. Relax. Take it easy. Go slow. Go with the flow of Source and love. Let everything be as it is and focus on how you want your life to be. Be easy, have fun, feel good. Go with general thoughts when things don't feel so good. Be specific when you do feel good. You got this. Be light about everything. Everything that you want is already manifested vibrationally, and it will show itself to you when you are in that place of feeling good, I promise. It is universal law and I know it to be so. Practice all this. These words are not the teacher, your life experiences are. Life is the ultimate guru. Trust yourself and listen to your emotional guidance system. You are never alone my friend, even when you think you are. Spirit, your guides, angels, your past loved ones, and many others are always with you, moving though you, guiding you, and are invested in everything you do. Remember to water your seeds and plants. Create and customize your daily spiritual practice. There are no days off. You will not want days off because it is so much fun to be in the flow and in alignment with who you really are, and when you are feeling the clarity of your life's purpose and why you have come!

May this book help you live this birth for all it's worth! May it help you customize your life and your spiritual practice. You now know how the universe works. You know how you work. You know about the Law of Attraction. You know how things manifest. You know why things are happening within you and around you. You now have the tools to do whatever it is you want. To heal what you want. To create what you want. You know how to meditate. You know how to be a mindful spiritual enlightened human being. You know where all your masks live and when you're wearing one or the other. You are now aware that there is much more to life than you thought there was. You can be in balance and harmony with the energy of Source and with nature.

May you experience all the healing and growth you need to live out your true life's purpose! You are ready. You can do this. I trust you. I believe in you. You're doing an awesome job! I hope to meet you one day soon and share a moment with you. Go forth, and be yourself. Be your true self. Trust yourself. Trust God. Trust your gut and your heart, for God and all your guides and helpers speak to you there. Everything you are looking for outside yourself can be found within your own heart and soul. Each day let your main intention be to feel good and have fun. If that is the only thing you take from this book, apply it and really mean it. It will be enough to transform your life forever. You can't get any of this wrong. You will never be done creating and will always desire to create more. Enjoy the ride. Easy come, easy go. Love fully. Live fully. Be mindful and present in the moment. Share your gifts and talents with the world. Don't hold back. Choose love over fear because fear is an illusion. Only love is true and real. May you find happiness. May you be healed and whole. May you have whatever you want and need. May you be protected from harm and free from fear. May you enjoy inner peace and ease. May you be awakened, liberated, and free in this lifetime! So be it, and so it is!

Thank you, I love you. Jai Ma!

: APPRECIATION :

I would like to give deep appreciation to the following:

Pete and Odie Florino, thank you for the world. Chris, Tino, and Neena thank you for always supporting me. My beloved Kriyanna Feyalove, the light of my heart, for your unconditional support and love. You inspire and assist me everyday in my self mastery and service to the world. Ari Powers for editing my book with such speed, dedication, and care. Abraham-Hicks, Mary, Jonathan, Centaur Sexy Horse Master, Zatar, Erabis, Toren and Snow Peace., and all the Ascended Masters I work with. All my guides, helpers, healers, past lovers, animal guides, angels, elemental beings, and ancestors. David Salmonson for always keeping me motivated and looking strong. All the healers and mentors I have be blessed to work with in my life including; Delores Van Lanen for transforming my life in all the best ways. Antoinette Saunders for always believing in me and always being so sweet and compassionate and thank you for helping me in such dark confusing times. Ascending Masters Council of Toren Collective. Stephanie, Sarah, Lisa, and Debbie Starnes for their unconditional love and inspiration to always shine bright! Noah Maze, Sara Strother, and Christina Corso for their wisdom and friendship. Cove School for teaching me how to be human, to all the students, fellow teachers, and friends that I did not mention that have been their for me and have influenced me in someway... Thank you. I love you all.

ABOUT MAHKAH DAS:

Mahkah's whole life has been passionately dedicated to going deep into his inner world to master himself. His intention is to live his birth for all its worth as an awakened, compassionate, mindful being. Mahkah is a 1,000+ hour certified Hatha yoga asana and meditation teacher along with being a Reiki Master and creator of Kaliguru sound healings. He is a teacher, a student, a mystic, a yogi, a lover, a father, a friend, and community leader. His goal is to help awaken the world into a state of alignment with Source energy. His endeavors support a vision of all humans living in ecstatic joy and love. Mahkah means Earth and Das means servant. Mahkah Das is committed to serving the Divine Mother and all of her children on this earth. Makkah is co-founder of Toren Collective in Portland Oregon where he lives with his beloved Kriyanna and their children.

Made in the USA
Charleston, SC
19 January 2017